Stand Up: Get in the Story
Published by Orange, a division of The reThink Group, Inc.
5870 Charlotte Lane, Suite 300
Cumming, GA 30040 U.S.A.
The Orange logo is a registered trademark of The reThink Group, Inc.

Other Orange products are available online and direct from the publisher. Visit our website at www.ThinkOrange.com for more resources like these.

Other Orange Devotionals:
Know God
Over the Fence

ISBN: 9781941259443

©2015 The reThink Group, Inc.

Writers: Dan Scott, Elizabeth Hansen
Editorial Team: Kristen Ivy, Mike Jeffries, Lauren Terrell, Laurin Greco, Tim Walker, Julie Tiemann
Art Direction: Ryan Boon, Sharon van Rossum
Illustration: Brian Bascle

Printed in the United States of America
First Edition 2015

1 2 3 4 5 6 7 8 9 10

04 / 19 / 2015

HEY THERE!

BOOK HERE.

What book, you ask? Why, the book you're holding, of course!

At this point, you're probably wondering: *What kind of book talks back to me? What kind of book did I just pick up?!*

Well, I don't blame you. Talking books are a little spooky. But before you throw me across the room and go screaming down the hall, there are a couple things you need to know about me.

First of all, **I'm not just any old book.** I'm not the kind of book you can check out from the library. I'm not the kind of book you can loan to a friend. I'm not the kind of book that'll get made into some Hollywood blockbuster movie. But that doesn't mean I don't have a story. In fact, I have something better—a lot of really great stories. But the second thing you need to know about me is, **I need *your* help to make me everything I was meant to be.** Like my title says, I need you to "get into the story."

Okay, okay, that's great and all but *which* story am I talking about?

> **The one about the Hero who saves the day?**
>
> **The one about a guy who's always doing the right thing?**
>
> **The one about the people who will stop at nothing to get the message out?**

Well, yes. Those stories and so many more.

And all those stories come together to make **ONE BIG STORY:** God's story. The coolest thing about God's story is it started thousands of years ago and He's not done writing it! In fact, He is inviting you to jump right into the action and I'm going to help you do just that.

I'm going to help you figure out ways to get into God's story by **standing up** for what's right . . . even when others don't.

That's conviction. And that's what I'm all about.

Think about it. You stand up for all kinds of things—like defending your favorite movie or song on the radio or arguing that your favorite pizza topping or ice cream flavor is the best.

And those are great and all, but . . . is that really what having conviction is all about?

Over the next eight weeks, I'm going to help you discover what it means to stand up for the right things. Through all kinds of cool stories, I'm going to show you how conviction sometimes means making wise choices. I'm going to show you that conviction has a lot to do with having the right friends. And I'm going to show you how important it is to trust God in order to **stand up** for what's right.

So, where do you start?

Glad you asked! Each week kicks off with a true story from the Bible—one of the stories that make up God's BIG story. After you read the story, you can jump right in to day 1 or start the devotionals the next day. Throughout the rest of the week, I've given you cool activities and deep questions based on what the Bible says about conviction. And don't skip the weekend page! (That may be my favorite!) That's where you'll find out how kids just like you are standing up for what's right all over the world.

Who knows, at the end of this book you might even find yourself with a big idea to **stand up** and change the world. All you have to do is get in the story!

What are you waiting for?! Go ahead, turn the page!

WEEK 1

STAND BY ME

JESUS IN THE GARDEN
MATTHEW 26:36-46

Everything that Jesus said and did amazed and astounded the people who followed Him. He said incredible things like, "*You have heard that it was said, 'Love your neighbor. Hate your enemy,' But here is what I tell you. Love your enemies. Pray for those who hurt you.*"

Once, Jesus healed a man who couldn't walk! But . . . He did it on the Sabbath. (Uh-oh . . .) Why was that such a big deal? Well, God had told His people not to work on the Sabbath, and the religious leaders thought Jesus was breaking God's rules by healing someone. What the religious leaders didn't understand is that healing someone's body isn't work—it's a celebration! It was one way Jesus showed people what God is like because Jesus is God. Still, the religious leaders believed He was upsetting everything. They became so frustrated and angry they plotted to get rid of Jesus when He came to Jerusalem to celebrate the Passover.

But Jesus knew exactly what the religious leaders were planning. (It's pretty tough to pull one over on Jesus.) So during the special Passover meal, He looked around the table at each of His friends. "*One of you will hand me over to my enemies,*" He told them.

After dinner, Jesus led His friends up the Mount of Olives. (That's just what they called the mountain—it wasn't actually a mountain made of olives. That'd be gross and hard to climb.) Moonlight cast long shadows across their path. "*This very night you will all turn away because of me,*" He cautioned.

Peter stopped in his tracks and shook his head fiercely. "*All the others may turn away because of you. But I never will!*" he claimed.

The disciples had seen Jesus' power. They couldn't believe anything bad was going to happen. After all, nothing bad can happen to Someone powerful enough to heal a man who couldn't walk! But even though Jesus was all-powerful, He knew there was something He had to do . . . and it was the last thing His friends expected.

After they arrived in the Garden of Gethsemane, He told His friends, "*Sit here while I go over there and pray.*"

Then He led Peter, James and John to a place where the roots of an ancient olive tree curled up from the ground. "*My soul is very sad,*" He said. "*I feel close to death. Stay here. Keep watch with me.*"

The three disciples quickly agreed to keep watch with Jesus. "You can count on us!" Peter declared.

As the three friends settled in between the rough tree roots, Jesus walked a short distance away. He knew what was coming and He could barely stand to face it. So He threw Himself down on the ground and cried out to God.

SIT HERE WHILE I GO OVER THERE AND PRAY.

"*My Father, if it is possible, take this cup of suffering away from me. But let what you want be done, not what I want.*"

As Jesus waited and listened, the chill of the night air seeped into His body. He stood and returned to His friends—only to find them sprawled out among the roots, sound asleep!

"*Couldn't you men keep watch with me for one hour?*" he asked Peter.

The men struggled to sit up, mumbling and rubbing their eyes.

"Wha—? Huh? I'm awake. I'm awake!" Peter gasped.

"*Watch and pray,*" Jesus warned. "*Then you won't fall into sin when you are tempted. The spirit is willing, but the body is weak.*"

Again, Jesus left His friends. He stumbled to His knees and poured out His heart to God.

"*My Father, is it possible for this cup to be taken away? But if I must drink it, may what you want be done.*"

The moon slid behind a cloud and the night darkened. Jesus rose from the damp ground and returned to His friends—who were sleeping again!

"Peter. James. John!"

They woke again as Jesus touched their shoulders. "Sorry . . . Didn't mean to . . . It has been such a long day . . ." John murmured.

"I'm dreaming . . . that I'm awake . . .," Peter mumbled.

JESUS HAD TO FACE WHAT LAY AHEAD ALONE.

None of them could keep their eyes open. Jesus had to face what lay ahead alone. Once more He left them and went a short distance away. With an aching heart, He fell to the ground and called out to God. He was so troubled that sweat poured down His face and dropped to the ground.

"*Father, if you are willing, take this cup of suffering away from me. But do what you want, not what I want,*" Jesus prayed.

A faint breeze rippled through the leaves of the olive tree. The moon silently slid from behind the clouds.

As Jesus lifted His face from the ground, He knew that God was giving Him strength. He would be able to follow through with everything that lay ahead.

One last time, He went back to His friends. Once again, Peter, James and John struggled to wake.

"Are you still sleeping and resting?" Jesus said. *"Look! The hour has come. The Son of Man is about to be handed over to sinners. Get up! Let us go! Here comes the one who is handing me over to them!"*

The three friends stumbled to their feet. "Handed over to who? What's going on?" Peter blustered as Jesus led His friends back to join the rest of the disciples. The truth quickly became clear as a crowd approached. Many of the men carried swords and flaming torches!

John frowned. "Jesus, we have to get you out of here. Let's leave Jerusalem."

"No way," Peter countered. "We'll fight! I'll take 'em out!"

Jesus shook His head and walked straight toward the angry mob. He knew exactly what was coming . . . and what God was giving Him the strength to do.

Jesus was arrested. He was put on trial. He was declared guilty even though He was innocent. And then Jesus, God's very own Son, was put to death on a cross.

But after three long days, God raised Jesus back to life! God had given His Son the strength to stand firm and follow through—even in the most difficult circumstances.

DAY 1

MATTHEW 26:36-46

BEFORE YOU GET STARTED TODAY, GRAB A BIBLE OR A BIBLE APP, A PEN AND THIS BOOK (OF COURSE!), AND FIND A NICE SHADY SPOT UNDER A TREE. IF IT'S RAINING OR THERE'S NO SHADE AROUND YOUR HOUSE, A NICE SPOT BY A WINDOW WILL WORK JUST FINE.

Open up to this page when you get there

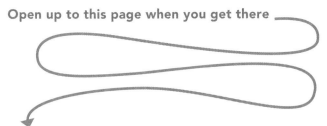

Oh, good! You're back!

Now, you may be wondering: *Why do I need to be outside for this? The beanbag chair in my room works just fine. Plus, it's super comfortable.* Well, take a look at Luke 22:39.

"Jesus went out as usual to the Mount of Olives."

As usual? Sounds like Jesus went outside to spend time with God a lot.

WHY DO YOU THINK JESUS MIGHT HAVE WANTED TO BE OUTSIDE WHEN HE PRAYED?

_____

_____

_____

HOW ABOUT YOU? WHAT VALUE DO YOU FIND IN BEING OUTSIDE OR LOOKING OUT AT THE WORLD GOD CREATED?

_____

_____

_____

According to Luke 22:39, Jesus went to the Mount of Olives often. So it probably wasn't too surprising when He asked His followers to join Him in the garden to pray.

But this time was a bit different. Jesus wanted to talk to God, His heavenly Father, about something *really* important—about dying on the cross. He was overwhelmed with what He needed to do. He could probably think of a million other things He would rather do. So He prayed and talked to God about it. You can read His prayer in Luke 22:42.

He knew He would suffer and feel pain. He asked God to make it so that He didn't have to die on the cross. But He also knew that He could trust His heavenly Father no matter what. So, He showed CONVICTION. He did what needed to be done—not because He wanted to, but because it was what God required for His plan to save the world from their sins.

When you choose to get in the story, God may ask you to stand up in a way that will take a lot of courage. Maybe you need to stand up for a friend who's being bullied or a teacher who isn't liked by the rest of the class. That's hard to do. But we can learn a lot from how Jesus showed conviction. Because Jesus showed us how to stand up for what's right.

He prayed. He trusted His heavenly Father to work everything out. And He obeyed. Most of the time, conviction is scary. But when it's the right thing to do, you can trust God will do great things with your willingness to stand up. Take a moment, while you're in or near creation, to ask God for the courage to stand up for what's right when the time comes. Ask Him for the peace, confidence and reassurance that comes with knowing you can trust Him no matter what.

JESUS SHOWED US HOW TO STAND FOR WHAT'S RIGHT.

DAY 2
1 JOHN 4:9-10

If someone asked you to prove something about yourself, how would you do it?

How would you prove you were a good soccer player or dancer?

How might you go about proving that pizza is your favorite food? Or that you love all things Disney?

Maybe you'd show them your moves, a tally of the number of pizza slices you consume in a given week, or your collection of Disney movies.

Easy. Right?

But what about the stuff that might be a bit harder to prove?

That you love your parents.

Or that you totally have the best BFF ever.

Those might be a bit more work, huh?

When Jesus was put on trial, He had done nothing wrong. He had told people who He was—the Son of God, the Messiah, the promised One who had been sent to rescue all people from their sin.

And even though what He said about Himself was true, it got Him in serious trouble.

People spit on Him and made fun of Him. They beat Him. And eventually they crucified Him.

Jesus was perfect. He *never* messed up. So why was He punished as if He did something *majorly* wrong? Well, one of Jesus' disciples, John, tells us.

GRAB YOUR BIBLE OR BIBLE APP AND READ 1 JOHN 4:9-10.

So why does John say Jesus let them do all that stuff to Him? Why did God let Jesus go through all that when He hadn't done anything wrong?

God sent His Son to save the world from sin. And you are part of the world, aren't you?

(You might see where I'm going with this.)

Jesus suffered through all that for you. Did you catch that? Jesus did all of that for you.

Doesn't that make you feel pretty loved?

Jesus knew that the only way you could be with God forever was for Him to go through all of that so He could pay for your sin. When He paid for your sin, He removed everything that kept you apart from Him.

That means that Jesus suffered through all of that horrible stuff because He wanted to.

Because He wants to be with you forever.

Because He loves you.

That might be hard to understand, but Jesus' love for us is sometimes hard to understand.

When Jesus stood for what was right, He proved He loved everyone.

He proved that He loves *you*.

That's why you can get in the story and stand up for what's right—because Jesus loves you very, very much. This week, find someone who knows a whole lot about Jesus. Ask them what Jesus' love means to them.

TAKE A MOMENT TO PRAY AND THANK GOD FOR THE AWESOME GIFT OF JESUS' LOVE.

DAY 3
LUKE 22:54-62

It wasn't supposed to be this way.

In Peter's mind, he figured he'd stand with Jesus until the very end. It didn't matter what Jesus had said about falling away; Peter thought that when the time came, he'd stand strong, show conviction and defend Jesus.

But that's not what happened.

You can read the whole story in Luke 22:54-62. Jesus had said that Peter would deny Him three times, and it all went down just like Jesus said it would. When people pointed out that Peter had been with Jesus, Peter denied ever even knowing Him.

GRAB A BIBLE OR BIBLE APP AND TAKE A LOOK AT LUKE 22:60-62.

WHAT DID PETER DO WHEN HE REALIZED WHAT HE HAD DONE?

Peter felt horrible. He must have thought he was the worst person in the world, and that no matter what, Jesus couldn't forgive him.

Has something like this ever happened to you? Have you ever known that you needed to show conviction by standing up for someone or something, but when the time came, you ran away? If it has, you're in good company. Even Peter, one of Jesus' closest friends, messed up.

But thankfully, it's not the end of your story. Just like this wasn't the end of Peter's story.

After Jesus rose from the dead, He forgave Peter and gave him a second chance, and Peter went on to be a leader in the church who stood up for Jesus no matter the cost.

Jesus gave Peter another chance. Jesus can give you another chance too. If you find yourself in Peter's shoes, it's easy to feel like you missed your chance to stand up for what's right. But talk to God about it. Tell Him how you feel. Ask Him to give you the courage to stand up the next time you find yourself in a similar situation.

TAKE A MOMENT TO WRITE OUT YOUR PRAYER ON THE NEXT PAGE.

DAY 4
LUKE 24:1-6

WHEN YOU HEAR THE WORD "EASTER" WHAT'S THE FIRST THING THAT COMES TO MIND?

You just wrote down "Jesus," didn't you? If so, great! You could practically write this book yourself! If not, well, join the club. How about a second chance?

WHAT'S THE *SECOND* THING THAT COMES TO MIND?

Still not Jesus? I get it. There's a lot of great stuff about Easter. Dinner, new clothes, baskets, Easter eggs, candy, chocolate bunnies, Peeps and jelly beans so good that it's hard to stop eating them until your stomach starts to churn.

Truth is, even if you know and believe that Easter is all about Jesus, it's hard to get past all the Easter candy and remember that Easter is about so much more.

Jesus' disciples had followed Him for about three years. They'd heard Him teach about the kingdom of God. They'd seen Him work miracles like walking on water, giving sight to the blind, and even raising people back to life. They believed He was there to rescue God's people—that's what God promised, after all! But Jesus was arrested and killed. Their hope—everything they had spent the last three years believing—was gone.

Three days later, a few women went out to the tomb where Jesus' body was. They went to give Him a proper burial, but what they actually found blew their minds!

OPEN YOUR BIBLE OR BIBLE APP TO LUKE 24:1-6 AND CHECK IT OUT. PAY SUPER CLOSE ATTENTION TO THE END OF VERSE 5 AND BEGINNING OF VERSE 6!

Did you catch that?

"Why do you look for the living among the dead? Jesus is not here. He has risen!"

The women had gone to the tomb thinking they would see Jesus' body, and instead they were told Jesus was no longer dead! Not only that, later they ended up seeing Jesus, eating with Him and celebrating that He was and is alive!

This devotional is all about getting in the story by standing up for what's right. And Easter—the celebration of Jesus' life, death and resurrection—is the best place to finish up the first week. Because this isn't just any story. This is God's story—the one He has been telling since the very beginning of time as we know it. And that story all points to Jesus, who He is, what He did for us on the cross, and how He came back to life! What a crazy and huge way for Jesus to stand up for what's right—to stand up for YOU!

Because Jesus stood up for what's right, you have a chance to get into God's story by standing up for what's right. You can stand up for what's right because Jesus already did.

Remember all those candies from before? See if you've got any jelly beans in the house or some other small Easter-type candy . . . maybe even left over from last Easter! ("Don't worry Mom—it's for my devotion!") THEN, USE YOUR JELLY BEANS TO CREATE A LITTLE REMINDER TO STAND UP.

1 Write the words "STAND UP" in big block letters on a piece of construction paper.

2 Using glue to secure them, fill the inside of the block letters with jelly beans.

3 After the glue dries, put your STAND UP reminder in a place you will see every day.

4 Whenever you see your STAND UP reminder, remember that you can stand up for what's right because Jesus already did.

DAY 5
MATTHEW 22:34-40

Let's start off with a few questions:

WHAT'S THE GREATEST MOVIE EVER MADE?

GREATEST SONG?

SPORTS TEAM?

BOOK?

FOOD?

DESSERT?

ANIMAL?

Those are great answers. Now, go find some friends or family members and ask them the same questions. Write their answers next to yours in a different color pen or marker.

(I'll wait) . . .

GREAT! NOW, COMPARE YOUR ANSWERS. HOW MANY WERE THE SAME?

Maybe a few of the answers—isn't pizza *everyone's* favorite food?!—were the same. But I'd guess that, for the most part, everybody's answers were completely different. That's because when it comes to stuff like food, movies and music, everyone has a different idea about what's the greatest.

Now, think about the Bible. There are *lots* of verses in the Bible—over 31,000 of them! And there are lots of commandments in the Bible too. God's people counted that there were 613 different rules they had to obey—and those were just in the first five books of the Bible!

Sheesh. That's a ton of rules. They were probably pretty hard to keep track of! One day someone asked Jesus, "Which rule is the greatest?"

And Jesus gave him an answer . . . He shared the one rule that is greater than all others.

GRAB A BIBLE IF YOU DON'T HAVE ONE ALREADY AND TAKE A LOOK AT MATTHEW 22:34-40.

(I'll wait) . . .

SO, WHAT'S THE #1 GREATEST THING? _____

_____

AND HOW ABOUT THE SECOND? _____

_____

Basically, Jesus was saying that everything God ever told His people to do—all 613 rules—could be summed up in two phrases: love God and love others.

We're going to spend the next eight weeks talking about what it means to stand up and get into God's story. And the Greatest Commandment—to love God and to love others—is a great reminder to keep focused on what standing up is all about. If you're gonna show conviction and stand up for something, stand up for what matters most: loving God and loving others. After all, it's the greatest thing you can do!

WEEKEND ONE

Standing for what's right and making a big change in the world can seem so overwhelming — especially when you're a kid. But Jesus showed us that standing up means just taking one small step at a time . . . and sometimes that can lead to something really big.

Craig Kielburger was only 12 years old when he began standing up against child labor—the horrible practice that enslaves 215 million kids worldwide. It was a *Toronto Star* newspaper article that changed Craig's life and sparked the conviction he needed to take a stand. The article Craig read as a 12-year-old boy in Toronto, Canada, was about another 12-year-old boy thousands of miles away who had lived a *very* different life than Craig.

Iqbal Masih was born in rural Pakistan. When he was only four years old, Iqbal's family sold him to a carpet factory as a child laborer in order to pay off a debt. Iqbal worked 14 hours a day, seven days a week with only one short 30-minute break per day. He was chained, along with the other children in the factory, to prevent escape. After six years of working in these extreme conditions, Iqbal's family's debt had only grown larger. There was no end in sight.

At age 10, Iqbal learned it was against the law in Pakistan to make children work off a debt. So he escaped and began speaking out against bonded labor. In just two years, Iqbal helped over three thousand children in Pakistan escape bonded labor. He began travelling the world, speaking about the issue in Pakistan and he completed the equivalent of four years of school. In just two years! Iqbal was making a *big* difference. Unfortunately, there were a lot of people in Iqbal's country who made a lot of money off child labor and didn't like the difference Iqbal was making. They didn't want other countries to start looking into the issue of child labor in Pakistan. So on April 16, 1995, when Iqbal was only 12 years old, he was shot and killed shortly after returning from a trip to America.

But Iqbal's work could not be stopped.

Thousands of miles from Iqbal's family in Pakistan, the *Toronto Star* covered the tragic story and another 12-year-old boy picked up Iqbal's campaign against child labor. When Craig Kielburger read the article written about Iqbal Masih, he knew he had to stand up for all the children like Iqbal. Craig didn't know where to start, so he took the article to school and gave a speech to his class about what he had read. He soon found that he wasn't alone in the conviction he felt. Eleven of Craig's classmates also wanted to help take a stand for Iqbal. And so, with no money and nowhere to meet other than Craig's living room floor, the students founded a group called the "Twelve Twelve-Year-Olds."

Just a few months later, Craig found himself travelling to Asia with a 25-year-old family friend from Bangladesh to see the conditions for himself. As it turned out, the Prime Minister of Canada (like the President of the United States) was going to be nearby in India at the same time. Craig asked if he could meet with the Prime Minister and when he was denied a meeting, 12-year-old Craig arranged a press conference to point out the "moral responsibility" of Canada's Prime Minister to take action against child labor.

That got the Prime Minister's attention!

Before long, Craig was meeting with Canada's Prime Minister and heading up an organization—now called "Free the Children"—that was getting international attention. Craig became the face of this movement that was quickly growing beyond the 12 twelve-year-olds and began doing interviews with various news stations all over the world. When Craig was asked during one of the interviews, "Why you?" Craig simply answered, "Why not?"

Today, Free the Children (www.freethechildren.com) is active in 45 countries around the world. It's a charity that raises over 30 million dollars a year. Free the Children builds schools, provides clean water, and connects rural craftsmen to world markets so their artwork can be sold and support their families. And if all that isn't impressive enough, Free the Children works with over two million volunteers—nearly all under the age of 18.

The great thing about Craig Kielburger's journey is that it started so small. It started with one 12-year-old boy reading an article in the newspaper. It started with one kid who couldn't help but stand up.

JESUS SHOWED US HOW TO STAND FOR WHAT'S RIGHT.

DANIEL TRAINED
IN BABYLON
DANIEL 1

Daniel was born into an important family in Judah. When Daniel was still a very young man, the Babylonian empire led by King Nebuchadnezzar conquered Daniel's land and God's people. Nebuchadnezzar made sure God's people wouldn't rebel by marching Daniel and many other young men from prominent families out of Judah and back to Babylon with him!

Daniel and his friends wondered whether they'd ever see their homes again. By the time they reached Babylon after a harsh, dusty journey, they were scared and confused. **But Daniel stayed hopeful and reassured his friends. "God will be with us, whatever happens!" he promised.**

Ashpenaz, one of the king's court officials, brought the best and the brightest men of the captured Israelites to the palace. King Nebuchadnezzar wanted these men to go through special training for three years. After those three years, they would be formed into the perfect servants for the king himself. Daniel was one of the ones chosen to be trained in this strange and unfamiliar land, chosen to serve a king who didn't believe in or worship the one true God. Three of Daniel's friends were chosen too.

As the first order of business, Ashpenaz took charge of Daniel and his friends, giving them new names to fit their new lives.

"Daniel?! Silly foreign names like that will never do here in Babylon." Ashpenaz scoffed. "You'll need new names—normal names. Like . . . Belteshazzar! Doesn't that sound better than *Daniel*?" Ashpenaz spat out Daniel's name with a sour face. Then he pointed to three of Daniel's friends. "And you three will be Shadrach, Meshach and Abednego. You'll learn our language, of course, and all the great Babylonian writings. This is the chance of a lifetime, boys! You are the envy of the world, being trained to be real Babylonian men."

Daniel frowned as he realized what was happening: the king wanted Daniel and his friends to study Babylonian culture so they would become like the Babylonians themselves. The king wanted them to turn their backs on all their customs, their culture, their *religion*. **He wanted them to forget they were God's people!**

BELTESHAZZAR! DOESN'T THAT SOUND BETTER THAN DANIEL?

But Daniel's friend, now named Abednego, was worried about something else at the moment. "Call me Abednego if you must, but you can also call me hungry. I'm about to starve here," he complained. "Any way we can get a bite to eat?"

"Of course!" Ashpenaz led Daniel and his friends to a table set with mouth-watering foods. "You're the king's honored guests. Help yourselves, my young friends."

Shadrach's eyes grew wide as he took in the long table piled high with the most decadent foods. "Mmm . . . steak . . . " he murmured, almost in a trance.

"Are those Babylonian buffalo bites?" Meshach asked in an overly excited pitch.

Abednego was nearly drooling as he looked at the desserts. "That cake's got at least nine layers!"

"Only the best!" Ashpenaz told them with a wink. "Straight from the king's table."

The food smelled incredible. But Daniel had a sinking feeling in his stomach. He pulled his friends aside. "Guys, the Babylonian king is trying to make us one of them. Let's not eat the king's food to remind ourselves that we're separate. We're different from the Babylonians. We are *God's* people."

Daniel's friends were troubled. Abednego saw David's point but wasn't quite on board. "We gotta eat something, man!"

"We can ask for different food," Daniel suggested. "Simple stuff to remind us that we're separate from these people and all of the king's luxuries."

WE ARE GOD'S PEOPLE.

Daniel and his friends tried to ignore the delicious smells wafting from the table as they turned back to Ashpenaz. "This all looks great," Daniel admitted. "But could we eat something that's not from the king's table? It doesn't need to be anything fancy."

Ashpenaz's face went pale. "*I'm afraid of the king. He is my master. He has decided what you and your three friends must eat and drink. Other young men are the same age as you. Why should he see you looking worse than them? When he sees how you look, he might kill me.*"

No matter what Daniel said, Ashpenaz was too scared to listen. Ashpenaz just knew the king would be on to him when Daniel and his friends started to look puny and malnourished. And the king wouldn't have any of his men looking puny! So Daniel approached the guard assigned to take care of them instead. "*Please test us for ten days,*" Daniel requested. "*Give us nothing but vegetables to eat. And give us only water to drink. Then compare us with the young men who eat the king's food. See how we look. After that, do what you want to.*"

The guard frowned, then shrugged. "Hmm. Well . . . if rutabagas are your thing . . .," he mumbled.

For ten days, the guard gave Daniel and his friends nothing to eat but veggies and water. They crunched away at the food on their plates.

"I could get into the habit . . . of cabbage," Daniel decided.

"I like broccoli . . . probably," Shadrach added.

"Pass the peas, if you please," Meshach asked.

But Abednego just groaned, "I need a hamburger!"

It wasn't easy saying "no" to the delicious foods the other young men ate. But at the end of ten days, the guard called everyone out, "Line 'em up!"

He strode past the other young men, surveying their faces and punching their shoulders. "Good, good. I can see you've been eating well. The king will be pleased."

But when the guard reached Daniel and his friends, the man stopped in surprise. "Whaaaa—? You've been eating rabbit food. But you look even better-fed than the others!"

Daniel smiled. **God had helped them grow strong, even without eating the king's food!**

"Okay, fine," the guard told them. "You can keep eating veggies and water."

God continued to give Daniel and his friends knowledge and understanding as they studied.

At the end of their training, they were brought before the king, who stared at them with hard eyes. "Let's see what you know. How many inches in a meter?"

"39.3701!" Shadrach announced quickly.

The king shot another question at Meshach. "What do you call a group of porcupines?"

"A prickle," Meshach answered immediately.

The king turned to Abednego. "How long does it take to poach an egg?"

"Two minutes and 41 seconds," Abednego told him without blinking.

The king was impressed. "How are you all so smart?"

Daniel smiled and told him, "The One True God gives us wisdom."

"Hmph," muttered the king. "Well, we'll see about that. Anyhow, you're ten times smarter than my other advisors. You'll serve me!"

Daniel and his friends joined the ranks of the king's advisors and eventually became his most trusted counselors. But though they served the King of Babylon, they never stopped standing strong for the one true God.

DAY 1
DANIEL 1

Let's say you have to make cookies for your swim team's bake sale tomorrow. But you don't have a cookbook or access to the Internet. (And, no, you can't just swing by the cookie section in the grocery store.) **Without looking anything up,** using only the information in your head, write down all the ingredients you will need and the instructions on how to make your homemade cookies:

INGREDIENTS: _____

_____

_____

INSTRUCTIONS: _____

_____

_____

_____

_____

Now, go find a cookie recipe (for the same kind of cookies you were trying to make) and compare it to your off-the-cuff recipe. How close are the two? What are the chances the recipe you originally wrote down would be as delicious as the recipe you found?

Okay, okay, that wasn't a fair test. How can you make a cookie when you've never read the recipe? Well, the same is true for standing up for what's right. How can you stand up for what's right when you've never read what God says is right?

The Bible story that started this week off is from the Old Testament. You can read all about that story and more stories about Daniel's life in the book of the Bible named after him. You guessed it—it's called the book of Daniel.

Daniel was just a young man when he and his friends were captured by King Nebuchadnezzar and taken from their home in Judah to Babylon. They were all super-smart, and King Neb wanted their talent for Babylon. He tried to do whatever it took to make them forget all about their home and the one true God.

He gave them new, hard-to-pronounce names: Belteshazzar, Shadrach, Meshach, and Abednego. And he tried to make them more Babylonian by giving them scrumptious, luxurious Babylonian food from the king's table. But even though Daniel was young, he knew better. He knew God didn't want them to be just like the Babylonians. God wanted Daniel and his friends to remember that they were His people!

Daniel knew what God said and how God wanted him to live. So Daniel stood up for what was right and made a deal.

GRAB YOUR BIBLE AND READ ALL ABOUT IT IN DANIEL 1:12-14.

How would you like to eat nothing but veggies for ten days? Yeah . . . I thought so. But after ten days, Daniel and his friends were stronger and healthier than all of the guys who feasted on the richest foods in Babylon. Because Daniel knew what God said, he was able to stand for what was right. He knew he could trust God no matter what.

So what do you think this means for you? Well, maybe you need to discover more about what God says in the Bible. Or maybe you already know a ton about the Bible and you just need to start putting it into practice.

Take a moment to pray and ask God to help you remember what He says is right. Then take a few minutes to WRITE DOWN A FEW THINGS YOU ALREADY KNOW GOD THINKS ARE RIGHT—bonus if you can write down the verse reference too!

1. _____

2. _____

3. _____

Then maybe you can bake some of your favorite cookies—just be sure to use the right recipe!

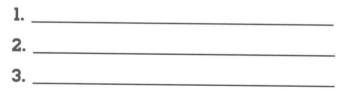

WHEN YOU KNOW WHAT GOD SAYS, IT CAN HELP YOU STAND FOR WHAT'S RIGHT.

DAY 2

HEBREWS 4:12

Fill in the blank with the first word or phrase that comes to mind.

THE BIBLE IS

What did you write? Long? Confusing? Really great? A book? God's Word?

Did you write that the Bible is a lamp? Or that the Bible is alive? Or that the Bible is sharper than a sword? . . . Chances are those weren't the first words that came to mind.

BUT GRAB A BIBLE OR BIBLE APP AND CHECK OUT HEBREWS 4:12.

It says, "*The word of God is **alive and active**. It's **sharper than any sword that has two edges**.*"

Uhhhh . . . alive? Is the Bible in your hands wiggling around? Is it dancing? Can you hear it breathing? Do you have to feed it twice a day?

And sharper than a sword? Have you ever tried to cut through a juicy apple with . . . your Bible?

Those words are pretty confusing and might not make a lot of sense when you first read them. So think about it this way.

The Bible isn't just a collection of stories or some old history book that sits on the shelf.

The Bible is God's message to us. The words on the pages of the Bible are the ones that introduce us to God and His great love for us. In the Bible we meet Jesus, God's Son and God Himself, who shows us exactly who God is—how He lives and loves. The Bible tells us the awesome true story of how Jesus came to earth and gave His life so that we could be with Him forever.

The words may have been written thousands of years ago but they still mean something to us in the twenty-first century. As you read God's Word, a lot of times you'll feel His love for you. And God will also speak to you through the Bible too! So the words aren't dead and meaningless. The words are **alive**! They speak to the hearts of people today just like they did when they were first written.

And even though the Bible might not be able to slice a McIntosh, it can cut deep inside of us—in a good way.

Have you ever read a passage of the Bible and felt like, "Oh, I shouldn't have lied to my dad yesterday." Or, "Yes! I knew that God would want me to share my snack at the pool today."

When we read the Bible, God often uses the words like a sword or knife to cut away the parts of our hearts and lives that don't line up with how He wants us to live. And He can also use the Bible to show us the great work that He is doing in our lives. He can use it to show us how He's growing us into the people He wants us to be.

But that's not all the Bible is or what it does. No, it doesn't stop there.

LOOK UP THESE VERSES TO FIND OUT WHAT ELSE IS SAID ABOUT THE BIBLE.

PSALM 119:105: The Bible is a _____

and a _____ .

MATTHEW 4:4: The Bible is _____ .

LUKE 8:11: The Bible is the _____ .

Ask someone in your home for some old magazines that you can cut up. Grab a pair of scissors, a glue stick and maybe some construction paper. Find words that describe the Bible and cut them out. Make a collage of these words. Hang the collage in your room where you'll see it. It can be a reminder to turn to God's Word when you're not sure how to show conviction.

DAY 3
2 TIMOTHY 3:12-17

POP QUIZ! Put a check in the box next to the things you should stand up for.

☐ **Your brother, sister or friend**

☐ **The last slice of pie**

☐ **A full hour of screen time after dinner**

☐ **Not having to make your bed**

☐ **Less homework on weekends**

☐ **Being kind to animals**

☐ **Five extra minutes at the park**

☐ **Respecting your mom and dad**

☐ **Listening to your music in the car**

☐ **Getting a driver's license at age 12**

Okay, pencils down. How do you think you did? Hard to tell? Some of those were easy—like standing up for your brother, sister or friend. That one should have been a no-brainer. But . . . should you stand up for your right to drive a car at age 12? Or wanting to listen to your own music? The truth is, the Bible doesn't *specifically* talk about all that stuff. ("Screen time" wasn't even a thing two thousand years ago!)

Sometimes it's hard to know what to stand up for. *When* should we show conviction? *How* should we show conviction? Will we know what to do when the time comes?

Back when the church first started (like nearly two thousand years ago), there was a young pastor named Timothy. Paul was Timothy's mentor. One day, Paul wrote Timothy a letter encouraging him to keep following everything he had learned from the Bible. You can actually read the whole letter because it's included in the Bible in the book of 2 Timothy.

"You have known the Holy Scriptures ever since you were a little child. They are able to teach you how to be saved by believing in Christ Jesus. God has breathed life into all Scripture. It is useful for teaching us what is true. It is useful for correcting our mistakes. It is useful for making our lives whole again. It is useful for training us to do what is right."

WRITE DOWN 5 THINGS THAT THE BIBLE IS USEFUL FOR OR CAN HELP US FIGURE OUT.

1. _____

2. _____

3. _____

4. _____

5. _____

And then you get to verse 17.

"By using Scripture, the servant of God can be completely prepared to do every good thing."

Did you catch that? *Prepared to do every good thing.* Paul is saying the Bible can help us know when to stand up and prepare us for how to stand up . . . even without saying the words "make your bed."

So when you're wondering about when you should stand up, head to the Bible. Learn some of the verses that tell us how to live and what we should stand for.

Grab that Bible again and do some digging. Find out what God wants us to know about showing conviction and standing for what's right!

Here are a few to get you started. **NEXT TO EACH REFERENCE, WRITE SOMETHING GOD WANTS US TO DO IN YOUR OWN WORDS.**

1 JOHN 4:11 _____

PROVERBS 12:22 _____

JAMES 2:1 _____

PHILIPPIANS 2:3 _____

PROVERBS 19:17 _____

And one last one . . . (Watch out, there's more than one in this verse!)

PHILIPPIANS 4:8 _____

Now . . . it's up to you. When you're not sure what to do, check out God's Word.

Maybe it doesn't talk about screen time specifically, but it does talk about being generous.

(So maybe you should share that screen with someone else.)

And maybe the Bible doesn't say anything about making your bed but it does talk about obeying your mom and dad. (So if it's important to them, God says it should be important to you.)

Just like Paul told Timothy, the Bible will give you everything you need to be completely prepared to do *every good thing*. *(See what I did there?)*

DAY 4
ACTS 2:1-12

Last week we talked about Peter denying that he even knew Jesus instead of standing up for what was right. But like we said, before He went back to heaven, Jesus gave Peter a second chance and told Peter that he'd be a leader in the church.

After Jesus went back to heaven, something amazing happened.

You might think you're reading a fable or a fantasy, but this is in the Bible. It really happened!

IF YOU WANT, YOU CAN READ IT FOR YOURSELF IN THE BIBLE IN ACTS 2:1-12.

Here's the quick version: The disciples were hanging out together when suddenly the whole house filled with a loud noise that sounded like a strong wind. Something that looked like tongues of fire appeared to rest on each person's head. The Holy Spirit filled them and soon they were speaking in languages they had never spoken before.

People from all over the world were in Jerusalem for a festival. And once they heard the loud noise, many people from many different places came to the disciples to find out what was going on. But no matter where they were from and what language they spoke, they could understand what the disciples were saying. They were amazed that these guys from Galilee could speak their languages. Everyone wondered what was going on.

Then guess who spoke up?

That's right, Peter! **The same guy who only a few weeks earlier had denied ever knowing Jesus was now speaking about Jesus to a crowd of thousands of people!**

He told everyone how God's Holy Spirit had come and given them the power to speak in these languages. He quoted one of God's promises from the Old Testament book of Joel. (He quoted Joel 2:28-32.) He talked about Jesus and His resurrection. He even told everyone that they needed to put their faith in Jesus too!

With the help of the Holy Spirit, Peter had the courage to stand up and share his faith with thousands of people. And guess how many people came to believe in Jesus that day?

(Here's a hint: check out Acts 2:41.)

Amazing, right?

Okay. So you might be wondering: *Cool story and all, but what does it have to do with me?*

Well, Peter experienced Jesus' love first hand. He knew what the Bible had said about Jesus and the promise of the Holy Spirit. All of that had come true. God kept His promise to the world. God kept His promise to Peter. Peter could have conviction because he could trust God no matter what.

And you can too. The Bible is full of promises about Jesus that came true. Over and over again God told His people that something would happen . . . and it did! No matter what you face, you can trust God to help you through it because He promises that He will. And He has been keeping His promises since the beginning of time!

TAKE A FEW MINUTES TO LOOK UP SOME OF GOD'S PROMISES IN THE OLD TESTAMENT THAT CAME TRUE IN THE NEW TESTAMENT. READ THE VERSES BELOW AND FILL IN WHAT WAS FULFILLED.

GENESIS 22:8 **JOHN 1:29**	
EXODUS 3:13-14 **JOHN 8:58**	
MICAH 5:2 **MATTHEW 2:1-2**	

(Answer Key: Lamb of God, The Great I AM, Born in Bethlehem)

Remember that you can stand for what's right because God keeps His promises.

DAY 5
LUKE 4:1-13

Sometimes conviction means that you need to stand up for people, but sometimes it means that you need to stand up to temptation. (Whoa. That's a big word.)

What in the world is temptation?

Well, you know that sneaky little voice inside your head that tells you it might be a good idea to pull your sister's hair, lie about your bad grades to your mom or download an app without permission?

I think you know what I'm talking about. That's temptation. And it sneaks up on you when you least expect it. It's a thought that tempts you to do something wrong, something you know you shouldn't do.

And conviction means standing up for what's right—even when you're just standing up to thoughts inside your own head. Because sometimes what you *want* to do might not be what's right.

You may be thinking it sounds pretty hard to stand up against . your own thoughts. But we can look to God's Word, the Bible, for help. As it turns out, Jesus Himself was tempted, and the book of Luke tells us how He fought against temptation in a really great and simple way.

YOU CAN FIND THE STORY IN LUKE 4:1-13.

So Jesus was in out in the desert where He had been fasting for 40 days. That's right—Jesus hadn't eaten anything for *40 days!* He was hungry, tired and weak, and that's when Satan made his move.

Satan tempted Jesus about three different things. And each time, Jesus knew exactly how to respond. Of course, Jesus is God, and He is perfect. But He stood up to temptation just like you can: **with God's Word**.

READ THESE VERSES FROM LUKE 4 AND WRITE DOWN HOW JESUS WAS TEMPTED:

LUKE 4:3 _____

LUKE 4:5-7 _____

LUKE 4:9 _____

Each time Jesus was tempted, He responded with verses He knew from Scripture. (That's just a fancy word for "the Bible.")

TAKE A MINUTE AND WRITE DOWN THE VERSES JESUS USED TO STAND UP AGAINST HIS TEMPTATIONS. But instead of looking them up in the story in Luke, take a little adventure into the Old Testament and discover the actual verses that Jesus quoted to resist temptation. Once you have read them, write them in your own words in the space provided.

DEUTERONOMY 8:3 _____

DEUTERONOMY 6:13 _____

DEUTERONOMY 6:16 _____

How cool is it that Jesus had memorized passages from part of the very same Bible you're holding now?! Well, maybe not the exact same leather-bound Bible or shimmery pink smart phone you're holding . . . but the exact same story! And by memorizing words from the Scriptures, He was able to fight back and stand up against temptation.

Think about all the verses in the Bible! Just like Jesus, when you get to know your Bible and discover all the great verses in there, the next time that sneaky little thought comes popping into your head, you can squash it like a bug and stand up for what's right.

One great way to learn verses from the Bible is to just start reading it and writing down verses that stand out to you! You could read it from beginning to end or you could start with one of these books: Genesis, Psalms, Mark, Acts, 1 Timothy

And for a quick start, here are some really great verses from the Bible to go ahead and start memorizing. Write them on notecards. Store them in your phone. Recite them before bed at night and at breakfast each morning.

1 Corinthians 10:13 "You are tempted in the same way all other human beings are. God is faithful. He will not let you be tempted any more than you can take. But when you are tempted, God will give you a way out. Then you will be able to deal with it "

Philippians 4:8 "Finally, my brothers and sisters, always think about what is true. Think about what is noble, right and pure. Think about what is lovely and worthy of respect. If anything is excellent or worthy of praise, think about those kinds of things."

Romans 12:9 "Love must be honest and true. Hate what is evil. Hold on to what is good."

WEEKEND TWO

The Bible has a lot to say about standing up for people in need. And when you start looking at the world around you, you'll quickly find many people in need. We know the Bible says we should stand up and help . . . but how?

Things like global hunger, starving children and malnutrition are big problems that seem way too overwhelming for a kid to tackle. How can you make a difference with a problem like world hunger when you aren't even old enough to make your own spaghetti?

Well, would you believe that every week thousands of kids come together all around the country to prepare, package and ship millions of meals to the poorest parts of the world? That's right! Each year, an organization called Kids Against Hunger sends out *40 million* meals to hungry children and families around the world.

Kids Against Hunger started out in 1999 and since its start has provided nearly 200 million meals in 65 different countries. **Here's how it works: Kids just like you show up at one of more than 100 locations around the country to volunteer their time and learn a little about global hunger.** They measure rice, veggies and vitamins, and put it all in a small, tightly sealed package that has a shelf life of three years. This package will feed six children when boiled.

Kids Against Hunger has created a very specific recipe that addresses the nutrition needs of people who are malnourished. In other words, it's not just crackers and sardines! This airtight, dehydrated "casserole" they ship out is made with 21 essential vitamins and minerals. They aren't just providing meals. They're providing better health.

And all through volunteers just like you!

But you might be surprised to find out that these packages aren't just shipped to poor, impoverished countries like the ones you see on TV. No, one-third of these meals are actually distributed in the United States. A recent study showed that over 16 million kids in the U.S. don't have enough food to thrive. **16 million!** That's like Michigan Stadium—the largest stadium in the U.S.—filled to the max *160 times!* And that's just hungry *children*. That doesn't take into account all the hungry adults and elderly people in the United States.

Still, as crazy big as that number sounds, the hunger problem in the U.S. is nothing compared to the rest of the world. If you were to just look at developing countries—or "third world" countries—you'd find 791 million people who aren't just "hungry" but are actually classified as "chronically undernourished." *791 million!* That's like Michigan Stadium filled to the max *7,900 times!* With seriously starving people. That means one out of every nine people in the world is starving.

That is absolutely mind blowing.

Kinda makes your mom's meatloaf sound scrumptious, doesn't it?

So, global hunger is a problem. But what can you, a kid, do about it? The answer is: *a lot!* How can *you* stand up against global hunger? Find a local Kids Against Hunger food-packaging center and volunteer your time. Or, if your community doesn't have a place like that nearby, visit **kidsagainsthunger.org** to find out how to start your own local satellite!

WHEN YOU KNOW WHAT GOD SAYS, IT CAN HELP YOU STAND FOR WHAT'S RIGHT.

WEEK 3

THE DREAM WHISPERER

DANIEL AND THE STATUE DREAM

DANIEL 2

King Nebuchadnezzar had chosen some very unlikely men to be his advisors—Daniel and his friends. Not only were they from a foreign land, but they believed in God, the one true God—and King Nebuchadnezzar had only ever worshipped the false gods of his culture. But the king was starting to admit there was something to worshiping this one true God. God had been doing some amazing things through Daniel and his friends. And King Nebuchadnezzar himself had said their counsel was ten times better than that of the other wise men.

But advising the King of Babylon was no piece of cake! In fact, there were times when it could be pretty dangerous to be the king's advisor . . .

Early one morning, the king woke up in a cold sweat. The strange images he had seen during his sleep still seemed to dance before his eyes. "I've had a terrible dream," he cried out. "I must know what it means immediately!"

He called to Arioch, the commander of the king's guard, and ordered: "Bring all my wise men at once."

Many of the king's advisors were called in, but Daniel and his friends weren't among them. At the palace, however, the wise men who *had* been called were wishing they'd never heard what the king had to say.

"King Nebuchadnezzar, may you live forever!" they flattered him, bowing low. *"Tell us what you dreamed. Then we'll explain what it means."*

The king narrowed his eyes; he didn't trust his advisors. "Not so fast," he warned them. "First, you tell me what I dreamed."

"That's impossible!" they declared.

"If I tell you what I dreamed, you'll just pretend you know what it means and make something up," the king pointed out. "So tell me what I dreamed and then explain it. If you do, I'll reward you greatly."

The advisors turned pale. *"There is no one on earth who can do what you are asking,"* they wailed. *"No king has ever asked for anything like that."*

The king narrowed his eyes even further, until they were mere slits. He was becoming so angry that the advisors jumped into action, shouting over each other as they tried to guess the dream. "Ahhh! Well in that case, you saw a bunch of parsnips . . . spinning golden flax into thread . . . while hanging out on the beach eating pomegranates and frogs' legs!"

"No, you fools!" the king roared. "Arioch, take these men away. Have all my wise men diced up into little bits!"

> # FIRST, YOU TELL ME WHAT I DREAMED.

Arioch and the king's guards began rounding up all the wise men, even those who hadn't been called in at first. This time, Daniel and his friends—Shadrach, Meshach, and Abednego—were on the list!

Daniel tried to keep a level head when Arioch brought the news. *"Why did Nebuchadnezzar give a terrible order like that?"* he asked.

"He thinks all the wise men are trying to trick him with fake answers," Arioch explained.

Daniel knew if someone didn't act, he and his friends and all the king's advisors would be killed. So he dared to go and speak with the king. "Your Majesty!" he pleaded. "I can help you understand your dream. But I need a little more time."

"Hmph," the king grumbled. Angry as he was, he really didn't want to lose all of his advisors in one fell swoop. So he backed down a tiny little bit. "Well if I recall, you're a sharper sword than the rest of these fools," he conceded to Daniel. "You've got until tomorrow."

When Daniel returned home, he gathered his friends and took a deep breath. "Pray and ask God to give me mercy and to help me understand the mystery of the king's dream," he asked them. "It's our only hope."

That night, God gave Daniel a vision—pictures that revealed the king's dream and what it meant. Daniel was overwhelmed with relief and thanked God immediately. *"May God be praised forever and ever!"*

The next morning, Arioch took Daniel to see the king again.

THAT NIGHT, GOD GAVE DANIEL A VISION

"Can you tell me what I saw?" demanded the king. "And what it means?!"

"You have asked us to explain a mystery to you. But no wise man can do that," Daniel explained. *"But there is a God in heaven who can explain mysteries.* In your dream, He has shown you things that haven't happened yet. In your dream, you saw a large statue. *And it terrified you. The head of the statue* was made out of pure gold. Its chest and arms were made out of silver. Its stomach and thighs were made out of bronze. Its legs were made out of iron. And its feet were partly iron and partly baked clay."

The king stared at Daniel in amazement. It was clear that Daniel had every detail exactly right.

"*While you were watching,*" Daniel continued, "*a rock was cut out. But human hands didn't do it.* It struck the statue and destroyed it all. The pieces blew away. But the rock turned into a huge mountain that filled all of the earth."

Then Daniel explained what the dream meant: God had given Nebuchadnezzar power. But his kingdom would end, and others would come after. In the end, God's kingdom would come, destroying all other kingdoms and lasting forever.

"The one true God has shown you what will happen," Daniel told the king. "You can trust the meaning I have given you."

When Daniel finished, everyone in the entire throne room was silent for a long moment. Then the king slowly rose from his throne and bowed low in front of Daniel!

"*I'm sure your God is the greatest god of all,*" announced the king. "*He is the Lord of kings. He explains mysteries.*"

Daniel took a deep breath and dared to ask, "So . . . you won't kill any of the wise men now?"

"Kill them?" roared the king. "No! I'm putting you in charge of them all. I'm making you ruler over Babylon and all the towns around it."

"That's a big job, Your Majesty," Daniel told him. "Could you appoint my friends to help?"

"Consider it done!" the king declared.

Daniel's friends, Shadrach, Meshach and Abednego, were also given positions of honor to help him, and together they served the king. They and all the wise men of Babylon were saved, because Daniel had dared to trust God.

DAY 1
DANIEL 2

Have you ever been given an impossible task? Or at least you felt that way?

Maybe a parent asked you to vacuum the entire house

or rake all the leaves in the yard.

Maybe it's washing an enormous stack of dishes

or taking down all the Christmas decorations.

Or maybe it was just cleaning up your room without stuffing everything under your bed.

Impossible, right?

Take a second and think of the most impossible task you've ever been asked to do. WRITE IT DOWN HERE:

A lot of tasks in life seem absolutely impossible when we start them. But usually, we get going and realize what seemed impossible was just really difficult. Well, several of the people in this week's story were given a task that was truly impossible. And if they didn't come through, they'd end up dead.

So not cool.

But this is where our hero, Daniel, steps in. He knew there was no way it was okay for the king to ask his advisors to do something impossible. And he knew that God could help him do the impossible. So Daniel went to the king and made a deal that helped the people who were in trouble and would get the king's impossible task done.

Win. Win.

Can you imagine how the other advisors felt when Daniel saved them from being killed? They must have thrown a huge party for him or bought him a brand new cloak or at least felt like they owed him their lives . . . because they kind of did! See, when Daniel stood up for what's right, he stood up for others.

Remember that "impossible" task you wrote about over there? In the end, did anyone help you complete the task? Maybe no one helped you rake the yard but maybe someone cheered you on, believed in you, or even brought you ice cold lemonade to keep you going. **WRITE THAT PERSON'S NAME HERE:**

Because that person stood up, you were able to complete an impossible task. Just like when Daniel stood up for what was right, he helped others complete an impossible task. Take a minute or two to thank that person for how they helped you. Maybe give them a call, write a thank-you note, or record a video with your cell phone.

And next time you feel like you need to stand up for what's right, remember, you aren't just standing up for what's right. You are standing up for others too.

DAY 2
LUKE 10:25-37

"Who exactly is my neighbor?"

It seems like a simple enough question, right? But when a religious leader asked Jesus this question, it came with a lot of implications. The religious leader had just quoted a Bible verse that says:

"'Love the Lord your God with all your heart and with all your soul. Love him with all your strength and with all your mind.' And, 'Love your neighbor as you love yourself.'"

And when he asked Jesus to define the word "neighbor," the religious leader was really wanting Jesus to assure him that he was loving the right people. He really wanted Jesus to say, "Well, your neighbors are other religious leaders. Your neighbors are the people who are easy for you to love."

That's how the religious leader wanted Jesus to respond. But Jesus rarely responded the way people wanted Him to.

Instead, Jesus answered with a story: the parable of the good Samaritan. Maybe you've heard it before. Maybe you haven't. Maybe you can barely pronounce the word Samaritan (suh-**mar**-i-tn). Either way, read through the story here.

(AND IF YOU REALLY WANT TO GO THE EXTRA MILE, READ THROUGH IT IN YOUR BIBLE IN LUKE 10:30-35.)

The Parable of the Good Samaritan

(Retold by me. In other words, don't quote me on this.
Read it for yourself.)

Once upon a time, there was this guy who set out on a very dangerous road known for shady characters who would jump out and rob unsuspecting travelers. Unfortunately, this was exactly what happened to the Jewish guy. He was robbed, beaten and left for dead.

A little while later, a priest who was traveling along the road noticed the Jewish man. This priest spent his life serving God. Do you think he stopped and helped the guy?

Nope. He didn't. Would you believe that he actually crossed to the other side of the road to make sure he didn't even touch the guy?

Next up was a Levite. A Levite also spent his life serving God. And while it's hard to believe, the same thing happened.

Two very religious people didn't want to get messy and help this poor guy dying on the road.

But then another man came along . . . **a Samaritan.**

Now, before we go any further, there's something you should know about Samaritans. They weren't very liked by the Jewish people. Jewish people didn't really get along with Samaritans. And Samaritans didn't really get along with Jewish people. But this Samaritan didn't care about all of that.

In fact, Luke 10:33 says . . .

"A Samaritan came to the place where the man was. When he saw the man, he felt sorry for him."

The Samaritan didn't just see the man and run away. He saw the man—who he wasn't supposed to like—and actually felt sorry for him. So the Samaritan went to work.

He took the injured Jewish man to an inn where he cleaned him up and bandaged him. He gave the innkeeper money to care for the man while he traveled. And more than that, he promised to return and pay for any other expenses the innkeeper would have because of caring for this guy. So the Samaritan went on his way, leaving the Jewish man in a safe inn with an innkeeper to look after him and nurse him back to health.

The end.

After Jesus finished this story, He turned to His audience of religious leaders and asked them a question: Out of those three guys in the story, who was the neighbor to the guy who was robbed?

The religious leaders had no other choice but to say that the Samaritan—the person they disliked—was the neighbor.

Whaaaaaaat?! So Jesus was telling them that their neighbors weren't just the people who were exactly like them, the people who lived like them, who wore the same things, who ate the same food, who believed the same things. Jesus was telling them that God didn't just want them to love the people who were easy to love. He was telling them to love people like *Samaritans*.

Just like Jesus told the religious leaders back in the day, *everyone* is your neighbor. God wants you to love and stand up for *everyone*. Because everyone can use some help every now and then.

MAKE A LIST OF FIVE PEOPLE WHO ARE EASY FOR YOU TO LOVE.

1. _____
2. _____
3. _____
4. _____
5. _____

NOW, MAKE A LIST OF FIVE PEOPLE YOU THINK GOD WANTS YOU TO LOVE AND STAND UP FOR.

1. _____
2. _____
3. _____
4. _____
5. _____

Be praying for all these people this week. And keep this list handy . . . you're gonna need it in a few days.

DAY 3
NEHEMIAH 5:6-7

Standing up and showing conviction can be something that happens in a moment. You hear someone use a word that isn't polite. You see someone take something that isn't theirs. You see a person or an animal in urgent need of help. In those times, you have to stand up right away. You have to decide to show conviction in an instant, in the moment.

Other times, however, conviction might take a bit of planning.

In the Bible, the book of Nehemiah tells a story about a man named—you guessed it—Nehemiah.

He was "the man" when it came to planning and thinking things through.

So when he learned about how the nobles and officials in Jerusalem were taking advantage of poor people, Nehemiah made a plan and put it into action.

OPEN YOUR BIBLE OR BIBLE APP AND CHECK OUT NEHEMIAH 5:6-7.

Did you catch that? Nehemiah said, *"I thought it over for a while."*

In other words, Nehemiah didn't rush into standing up and showing conviction. He didn't want to go in and just start yelling at people. He wanted to make sure he had a plan—a plan that would really help. He wanted to make sure that he knew exactly what needed to be done.

And guess what? Nehemiah's plan worked. He was able to help make things right between the rulers and the poor people because he took the time to make a plan and then put it into action.

So what about you? Are there any plans you need to put into action? Yesterday, you made a list of people who could use your help. Choose one or two of those people. Think about what kind of help they need. Then, come up with a plan.

Ask a parent, adult or friends to help you if you need it. Together, figure out a way to stand up for others this week.

WRITE OUT YOU PLAN ON THE NEXT PAGE.

MY PLAN:

WHAT DO I NEED? _____

_____

_____

_____

WHO CAN HELP? _____

_____

_____

_____

WHAT STEPS CAN I TAKE TO MAKE THIS HAPPEN? _____

_____

_____

_____

_____

_____

_____

_____

DAY 4
ACTS 9:26-28

Have you ever done something wrong?

Okay, what am I saying? Of course you have! We all have. (Don't worry, I'm not going to make you write down the worst thing you've ever done.)

What I mean is, have you ever done something so bad it made someone unable to trust you? Maybe you lost a good friend because of it. Or maybe you lost some of your privileges at home. Either way, was it hard to earn that trust back? Were you ever able to earn that trust back?

Maybe you can think about it the other way too. Has anyone ever done something so bad—maybe they hurt you so deeply—that it made you totally unable to trust them again? Did that person change and try doing things to earn back your trust? If so, was it easy for you to trust that the person had actually changed?

Well, this is exactly what happened to the guy in today's story.

There was this guy named Saul. (You might recognize him by the name he was later known by—Paul the Apostle.) Saul was the self-appointed archenemy of the church. He made it his life's mission to stop the followers of Jesus from spreading Jesus' message. He wanted to arrest them, throw them in prison and even have them killed!

But then, Saul had an amazing encounter with Jesus. And he was like a new man. Jesus told Saul that he'd be *the guy* to take Jesus' message of salvation to the whole world.

For Saul, everything changed.

He went from persecuting Christians to *being* a Christian. Not only that, he went from trying to stop the spread of the good news of Jesus to being the person who actually spread the news all over the world!

He went from Saul the cruel to Paul the cool!

But for the disciples, well . . . it would take a little more convincing. It was hard for them to believe that this guy who'd wanted to *kill them* just a little while earlier was now on their side and joining their mission.

Except for one guy. His name was Barnabas. God had told Barnabas the truth about Saul. He knew how Jesus had met Saul in a major way. And Barnabas knew that encounter with Jesus had changed Saul—for good. So Barnabas decided to *stand up* for Saul and defend him to the rest of the disciples.

CHECK OUT WHAT HAPPENED IN ACTS 9:26-28.

Because Barnabas stood up for Saul, Saul was able to start his mission alongside the disciples and speak with conviction about Jesus.

What about you? All week, you've been making lists and planning to help some people around you. Maybe it's time to put your plan into action!

What's the first step you can take towards standing up for others in a major way? Does it mean volunteering some weekend time? Or raising money in a unique way? Whatever that first step is, take good mental notes about the experience. Oh! And take a selfie with the person you're helping (and anyone who's helping you too)! **In the space below, TAPE YOUR SELFIE INTO THE BOOK AND WRITE DOWN EVERYTHING YOU CAN REMEMBER about the time you spent standing up for someone!**

[TAPE SELFIE HERE]

_____

_____

_____

_____

_____

DAY 5
ACTS 16:16-40

We all know standing up for what's right is *hard*. Like climbing-Mount-Everest hard. But there's a little piece of us that believes if we stand up for what's right and do the right thing, it'll all turn out okay, right?

Have you ever experienced a time when you showed conviction and felt like it all blew up in your face? Like maybe you went to your mom about something your brother did wrong and ended up being the one to get in trouble? Or you stood up for someone who totally didn't appreciate it?

If that's happened to you (or even if you could imagine that happening), **take a minute to WRITE DOWN A FEW WORDS OR PHRASES about how that might make you feel** (like *irritated* or *embarrassed*).

_____

_____

If anyone knows how it feels to have conviction backfire, it's Paul and Silas. They stood up for someone in a *big* way and got thrown in *prison* for it!

You can read the story for yourself in Acts 16:16-40. It's a bit long, so here's a quick rundown.

There was a girl who was a slave. The people who owned her made money from her suffering. It was awful, but God used Paul and Silas to rescue her. She was free, but her owners were furious with Paul and Silas. They were angry because they couldn't make money anymore. So these men caused such a stir that Paul and Silas were thrown into prison.

Now, you'd think that Paul and Silas would be all angry and upset for being thrown into prison for helping someone who needed help. (I know I would be.) But Paul and Silas were different. God's Holy Spirit gave them joy even while they were in prison.

Don't believe me? Read it for yourself. Check out Acts 16:25:

About midnight Paul and Silas were praying. They were also singing hymns to God. The other prisoners were listening to them.

And then something incredible happened! And you need to read this for yourself.

GRAB A BIBLE AND READ ACTS 16:26-34.

Paul and Silas were in the worst situation. But they responded with joy. And because of that, the jailer and his entire family came to know Jesus.

This story is a great reminder for us. We can have joy even when standing up gets hard. Because . . . it's going to be hard. That's pretty much guaranteed.

So how can you have joy when standing up gets hard? Here are a few ways to get you started:

PRAY. Tell God about what you're feeling. It's the best way to help you get focused on His goodness rather than your problems.

READ THE BIBLE. The Psalms are a great place to start. Many of the songs and poems in the book of Psalms were written by a guy named David when he was going through some really hard stuff. He wrote a lot about how we can trust God no matter what we face. Try reading Psalm 11 or 13.

WORSHIP. Music is a great way to remind us of how awesome God is. Listen to a worship song that puts you in a better mood and reminds you why you stood up in the first place!

BE CREATIVE. You may find joy in writing a song or a poem of your own. Okay, that might sound like crazy talk. (Write a poem—are you nuts?!) But keep it simple. Just write down some ideas about God and how awesome He is. And guess what? It doesn't even have to rhyme! (It's totally your poem after all.) In fact, why not give it a try right now?

In the space below, **CREATE A POEM OR SONG** about finding joy when things don't go as planned. Who knows? You might be a poet and not even know it. *(See what I did there?)*

_____

_____

_____

_____

_____

_____

_____

_____

_____

WEEKEND THREE

There are a lot of people out there who don't have the courage to stand for what's right. But the good news is, you do! And when you stand up for what's right—when you show conviction—you're standing up for others, too!

When Jaylen Arnold was eight years old, he was no stranger to being bullied. Kids in his class laughed at the strange way he jerked his head. They called him horrible names because of the weird noises he made. While Jaylen *looked* like any other eight-year-old boy, he sometimes didn't act like everyone else. Jaylen had been diagnosed with Tourette's Syndrome, which meant sometimes he couldn't control his voice or body. He would make abrupt movements or strange shouts and noises without being able to control it. Jaylen was different from the other kids. And Jaylen quickly discovered that bullies don't like different.

But at eight years old, Jaylen knew bullying was wrong! He knew the kids in his class shouldn't be making fun of him, so Jaylen decided to stand up and do something about it. With the help of his parents, Jaylen made a simple website for the kids in his school. The website educated his peers about bullying—how hurtful and dangerous it was. Jaylen had the support of his parents and a few good friends but he knew many, many other kids were being bullied and had no one to turn to. Jaylen wanted to give those kids a voice. He wanted everyone who was being bullied to know they weren't alone and that they could join him in standing up against bullying! And so with that simple website, initially intended for his classmates alone, the internationally recognized charity, Jaylen's Challenge Foundation, Inc., was born. When he was nine years old, Jaylen began touring the country talking to kids his age about bullying. Jaylen began making wristbands with the phrase, "Bullying No Way!," impressed on them. These wristbands are worn by all kinds of celebrities. Not only that, Jaylen has been featured on news networks like ABC, NBC and CNN!

Jaylen says over the years, he's gotten hundreds of letters from kids who have been bullied and are choosing to take a stand. He has even heard from some of his own bullies who have come to him and apologized for making him feel so bad. But Jaylen says his favorite people to hear from are bullies from around the country who come to him to let him know they recognize how damaging and dangerous their words have been. He says there's no better feeling in the world than hearing how his efforts have changed the hearts of those bullies. Jaylen would have been thrilled to save just one kid from being bullied but by deciding to stand up and take action, Jaylen has touched *thousands* of lives!

Maybe you've been bullied. Maybe you've seen someone else being bullied. Or maybe you've been the bully—saying cruel things and laughing at others. The easiest thing to do is ignore it. Pretend it's not happening. But that's not the approach Jaylen took. Jaylen knew it was bullying and he knew bullying was wrong. Jaylen stood up for what was right and has not only made a difference for the kids in his own school but for 120,000 other kids too!

So how can you stand up against bullying? You can start by checking out **jaylenschallenge.org** where there's a bunch of great info on how to stand up against bullies, including a way to get Jaylen to come to your school! There are also smaller and very effective ways of standing up against bullying. If you see something mean on social media, *don't spread it!* Maybe you didn't post it. Maybe you aren't the target. But you can do your part by not bringing any more attention to it. And when you notice someone is the target of bullying, approach them with kindness. Let that person know you see how badly they're being treated. Let that person know you don't think it's okay and that you're on their side. Be a friend to someone who may feel alone. And as always, get an adult involved. Let a grown-up know if you see bullying happening or if you're the target of a bully. **Take a cue from Jaylen and don't just sit by and watch—stand up against bullying!**

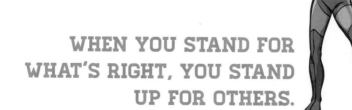

WHEN YOU STAND FOR WHAT'S RIGHT, YOU STAND UP FOR OTHERS.

WEEK 4

IF YOU CAN STAND THE HEAT

THE FIERY FURNACE
DANIEL 3

Remember the Bible story from week two? The one where Daniel and his friends are taken from Judah and marched to Babylon to work for King Nebuchadnezzar?

Good. Because we're picking back up with them this week—in Babylon.

Shadrach, Meshach and Abednego (remember those crazy names the Babylonians gave Daniel's friends?) had been appointed to high positions. They advised the king and helped to rule Babylon and the areas around it. But even though King Nebuchadnezzar had been impressed by the one true God they worshiped, he still believed in false gods too—even ones that he created! **It's one thing to make a *really* impressive and intricate structure out of your JELL-O after dinner. But it's something else entirely to declare your JELL-O statue a *god*!**

But that's exactly the kind of thing King Nebuchadnezzar did.

"Make me a statue 90 feet tall and nine feet wide," he ordered his finest craftsmen one day. "Make it out of solid gold!"

The craftsmen set to work melting gold in a blazing hot furnace and shaping it inch by inch into the imposing form of a massive giant. When the statue was completed, the king ordered that it be set up on the broad, flat plains of Dura. "Call all my advisors and officials from all over to come stand before the statue!" he demanded.

Soon, all of the king's officials and wise men gathered before the towering statue. Shadrach, Meshach and Abednego stood among them and stared up . . . and up . . . at the gigantic statue that gleamed far above them in the hot glare of the sun.

"I don't like this," murmured Shadrach.

"I smell trouble," Meshach agreed.

"We could land in hot water," Abednego warned.

The king's messenger called out to all the gathered officials and advisors, "*Listen, you people who come from every nation! . . . Here is what the king commands you to do.*" He took a deep breath and rattled off the order. "*You will soon hear the sound of horns and flutes. You will hear zithers, lyres, harps and pipes. In fact, you will hear all kinds of music. When you do, you must fall down and worship the gold statue. That is the statue that King Nebuchadnezzar has set up. If you don't, you will be thrown into a blazing furnace right away.*"

Daniel's friends exchanged worried glances. They worshiped the one true God alone. There was no way they were going to bow down to some golden oversized action figure!

"Strike up the band!" cried the messenger. Immediately, wild and beautiful music filled the air. Every single official and advisor fell flat on his face—except for Shadrach, Meshach and Abednego. They stood tall. And some of the other wise men noticed.

"It's those upstart Israelites who got promoted over us!" they grumbled. "We'll make sure they get promoted somewhere hotter."

YOU MUST FALL DOWN AND WORSHIP THE GOLD STATUE.

The advisors hurried straight to the king. "*King Nebuchadnezzar, may you live forever!*" they said as they approached His Majesty. "*You commanded everyone to worship the statue when they hear the music. But those Israelites—Shadrach, Meshach and Abednego—are refusing to worship your gods and your statue!*"

The king burned with anger. How could a handful of foreigners dare to disobey the orders of the most powerful man in the land? He immediately sent for Shadrach, Meshach and Abednego.

"Why aren't you worshiping the statue I set up?" he demanded. "When you hear the music, you must fall down in worship. If you don't, you'll be thrown into a blazing furnace. No god can save you then!"

Shadrach took a deep breath and met the king's eyes as he spoke for all three men. "*King Nebuchadnezzar. . . We might be thrown into the blazing furnace. But the God we serve is able to bring us out of it alive. He will save us from your power.*"

THE GOD WE SERVE IS ABLE TO BRING US OUT OF IT ALIVE.

Meshach jumped in to support his friend, adding, "*But we want you to know this, Your Majesty. Even if we knew that our God wouldn't save us, we still wouldn't serve your gods. We wouldn't worship the gold statue you set up.*" Meshach stopped for breath as Abednego and Shadrach both nodded in agreement.

The king could contain his irritation no longer. "Guards!" he demanded. "Make the fire seven times hotter. Tie up these men and throw them into the furnace."

Immediately, soldiers grabbed the three friends and tied them with thick ropes. Then they tossed them straight into the heart of the fire! The king was still enraged. "That'll teach 'em who's in charge!" he roared and glared into the flickering fire.

But just as quickly, he hurried as close to the scorching flames as he dared, an astounded look on his face. "Wait! *Didn't we tie up three men?*" he asked, peering into the raging furnace. "*Didn't we throw three men into the fire?*"

"Sure did!" his wise men agreed, still smug. They had not yet bothered to look into the fire themselves.

But the king couldn't tear his eyes away from the furnace. "*Look! I see four men walking around in the fire. They aren't tied up.*

And the fire hasn't even harmed them."

"Wait, what?!" one of the wise men exclaimed. All the advisors rushed toward the furnace, stopping only when the heat hit them like a wall. "But there were only three men!" cried one of the others.

King Nebuchadnezzar was mesmerized as his eyes continued to fix on the flames. *"The fourth man looks like a son of the gods,"* he exclaimed, approaching the mouth of the furnace. *"Shadrach, Meshach and Abednego,"* he called, *"Come out! You who serve the Most High God, come here!"*

The three friends came out of the furnace, completely unharmed. They smiled at each other, and then turned to present themselves to the king.

The wise men gaped and whispered among themselves. "Their hair didn't burn. Or their clothes! They don't even smell like they've been hanging out at a bonfire."

The king threw out his arms to welcome the men he had so recently condemned to die. *"May the God of Shadrach, Meshach and Abednego be praised! He has sent his angel and saved his servants. They trusted in him. They refused to obey my command. They were willing to give up their lives. They would rather die than serve or worship any god except their own God. No other god can save people this way."*

The king turned to glare at his other advisors. "I'm giving an order. No one from any nation can say anything bad about the God of Shadrach, Meshach and Abednego. Or they'll be diced up into little pieces!"

Instead of bowing down, Shadrach, Meshach and Abednego had chosen to stand for what was right. And the king was so amazed by the power of the one true God that he promoted the three friends to even higher positions in the kingdom of Babylon.

DAY 1
DANIEL 3

So . . . if you were Shadrach, Meshach or Abednego (you can choose whichever one you want to be), what would *you* have done?

No, really. Think about it.

You've been commanded to bow down to and worship a golden statue of the king, and if you don't, you'll be thrown into a giant fiery furnace.

Take a second, close your eyes and really try to imagine the statue, the king, the other people gathered around, the music playing . . .

It's a pretty scary thought, isn't it? Having to choose between disobeying God and burning alive. You probably can't even imagine what you would do if you'd been one of those three guys. Thankfully, you've got a pretty good chance this kind of thing won't happen to you. Whew!

But even though you probably will never be put in a situation where you have to choose between standing up for God and some sort of physical torment, you'll most likely be put in lots of situations where it still isn't easy to stand up for God. And when those times come, there's a lot of comfort and confidence that you can find in the way Shadrach, Meshach, and Abednego responded.

Let's review.

King Neb says: "Worship my golden statue! *Now!* Or I'll throw you into the fiery furnace!"

Shad, Mesh and Abe are like, "Uh, no way dude."

So King Neb goes, "No, seriously, I reaaalllly want you to."

Shad, Mesh, and Abe stand strong. "Nu uh. Not happenin'."

King Neb screams and stomps his feet. "Do it! DO IT! DOOOO IIIIIITTT!"

Shad, Mesh and Abe are like: "Yeah, we're not gonna do it. And you can throw us in that furnace all you want, but our God is big enough and powerful enough to keep us safe from any scary fire. And even if we knew He wouldn't save us from the flames, we still wouldn't worship your silly statue."

Okay, so that's a pretty loose version of the story but did you catch what the three friends said about not worshiping the golden statue *even if* they knew God wouldn't save them from the fire?!

Now that is serious standing up!

It's pretty easy to stand up for a God powerful enough to get you out of any sticky (or scorching) situation. But God never promised Shadrach, Meshach and Abednego that He would save them from any harm. And He never promises us that either.

It's just up to us to stand up for what God says is right and trust God no matter what.

The good thing for Shad, Mesh and Abed though, is that God really *did* show up in a big way that day to save them from the fire! By standing up for God, the three friends created a way that God could be shown to everyone in Babylon in a really impressive manner. After that, the people of Babylon really thought twice before messing with Shad, Mesh and Abed's one true God. And even cooler than that, King Nebuchadnezzar himself said that our God is a God to be praised!

So while you might not face a blazing furnace, you sometimes will face consequences for standing up for what's right.

WHAT ARE SOME OF THOSE CONSEQUENCES?

_____

_____

_____

The consequences are real . . . and sometimes really scary. But just like Shadrach, Meshach and Abednego, when you're brave enough to stand for what's right (even in the face of these consequences), it shows others that God is big and worthy of our praise!

Think of some songs that remind you just how awesome our God is. CREATE A PLAYLIST of those songs and play it when you think you aren't brave enough to stand up for what's right. Remember, you can trust God no matter what. And when you stand up for what's right, others can see God.

DAY 2
1 KINGS 18:1-39

Today, you'll need a parent or an adult for this first part. Go on, find one! (Preferably one you know.)

Okay, now ask that adult for a candle. Watch as the adult lights the wick of the candle or have them help you light it. Lights pretty quickly, doesn't it?

Now, blow out the candle. Then grab some water and get the wick all wet, like *really* wet. Maybe even hold it under the water for a while.

Try lighting it again. (Again, with adult supervision!)

Pretty hard, huh? It doesn't light right away. Sure, it sparks a lot, but getting it to actually light and *stay* lit, is *way* harder when the wick is wet.

Back in the Old Testament, there was a false god called Baal. In 1 Kings 18, God's prophet, Elijah, challenged Baal's prophets to a test to prove that God is the one true God, not Baal.

It was a god standoff. **Whichever god set fire to their sacrifice first was to be proclaimed the one true God.**

Baal's prophet set up their sacrifice—a bull on some wood. Baal's prophets spent hours and hours trying to get their god to set their sacrifice on fire, but nothing happened. Not even so much as a spark. Even Elijah joked around that maybe their god was busying going to the bathroom. (No, really! He said that! See for yourself in 1 Kings 18:27.)

Finally, they gave up. It was Elijah's turn. Elijah set up his bull on some wood and stones, but then he did something totally unexpected. Elijah raised the stakes even higher.

CHECK OUT WHAT HAPPENED IN 1 KINGS 18 VERSES 32-35.

The sacrifice, the altar, *everything* was completely drenched in water. They poured so much water over the sacrifice that there was a ditch full of water around it! Remember, Baal's sacrifice was still sitting there untouched—it wasn't lit on fire—and no water was involved. How in the world was Elijah's soaked sacrifice going to burn?

Well, Elijah knew that God is the only true God. Elijah knew he could trust God no matter what—even when it seemed absolutely impossible.

KEEP READING IN 1 KINGS 18:36-38.

And, man, did God show up!
Fire came down from heaven and in a flash the sacrifice was gone. Not just the sacrifice, but the water, the stones, the wood—*everything* was destroyed in the fire.

And in that instant, all the people fell to the ground and worshipped God—even Baal's prophets!

Pretty amazing, huh? But that's God. He's pretty amazing.

Imagine what everyone thought when the people doused God's altar with jar after jar of water. They must have laughed in his face! (Just like you might have when I told you to light that wet candle on fire.) But Elijah knew he could trust God to do the impossible.

You can take a risk and stand up knowing that God is all-powerful. Sometimes it seems impossible to stand up, but when you stand up for what's right, you can trust God to help you get through the impossible.

DAY 3
1 SAMUEL 17

Chances are, if you've been around church a while, you might have heard this story before. It's probably one of the top ten most told stories in the Bible. Maybe even if you haven't been in church before, you've heard this true story about a kid and a giant.

Nope. Not Jack and the Beanstalk—although that's a really great story. But, one, it's not in the Bible. And, two, it's not even close to true. Sorry.

The story I'm talking about is David and Goliath. It's a pretty great story, even if it is one a lot of people have heard before. It's worth hearing again, because it's a perfect example of standing up for what's right.

If you remember hearing the story before, try to DRAW A PICTURE OF IT in the box below!

If not, no big deal—you can find the whole story in 1 Samuel 17, but here's the gist of it . . .

God's people, the Israelites, were in a battle against one of their enemies. And among their enemies there was this guy, a giant—Goliath. He was huge—like *nine* feet tall! Every day for forty days, Goliath would come out and taunt God's army. The problem was, the Israelites were terrified of Goliath. It was like they forgot *they were God's people*! God could easily help them beat Goliath and their enemies. They could totally trust Him to defeat their enemies.

But they didn't. They freaked out and hid.

Then this young boy, David, showed up to give his big brothers some food. While he was delivering the food, he heard Goliath threatening the Israelites. David got mad. He couldn't believe that the Israelite army wasn't trusting God to rescue them from this giant. Plus, by insulting God's people, he was insulting God! So David decided to step up and take care of it himself.

But what's cool is that David didn't just stand up to Goliath to show everyone how cool and brave he was. Check out what David says at the end of 1 Samuel 17:46.

"Then the whole world will know there is a God in Israel."

David wanted to defeat Goliath not so he could become famous. He wanted to defeat Goliath because he wanted God to become famous. David stood up to Goliath, not with a sword or a spear, but with five stones and a slingshot.

And wouldn't you know it . . . that first stone hit Goliath square in the head and he fell down dead. With God's help, David defeated Goliath. Maybe if the whole army had attacked Goliath together, maybe if David had been a little larger himself, God's miracle wouldn't have been so obvious. But David was just a little kid . . . up against a *huge* giant. It was obvious God had a hand in the victory and everyone praised God for what He had done. (They might have thanked David a little bit too.)

Sometimes it might seem like you're standing up to a giant. Okay, not an actual giant, but sometimes things happen and it takes a *ton* of courage to have conviction and stand up for what's right. Maybe a kid twice your age is picking on your little sister. Maybe an adult seems to be doing something that's not right. Maybe there are rules in place that have been in place for a *long* time but don't seem to follow what God says is right.

TAKE A MINUTE TO JOT DOWN ONE OR TWO "GIANTS" IN YOUR OWN LIFE:

_____

_____

_____

NOW TAKE A SECOND TO DRAW A PICTURE OF WHAT IT MIGHT LOOK LIKE FOR YOU TO STAND UP TO YOUR "GIANT."

Standing up to your giant isn't going to be easy. It's going to take a lot of courage. So spend a little time today asking God to help you trust Him no matter what. And ask Him to use you to defeat the giants in your world.

TRUST GOD.

STAND UP.

DEFEAT GIANTS.

BOOM. Now . . . go do it!

DAY 4
JOHN 13:34-35

Grab a timer. Set it for three minutes. Now, **SEE IF YOU CAN COME UP WITH 25 PEOPLE YOU LOVE.** (It doesn't have to be mushy, gushy love. It can be the way you love your grandma or the way you love your best friend. Or the way you love that guy who works at the hot dog stand who always gives you extra relish.)

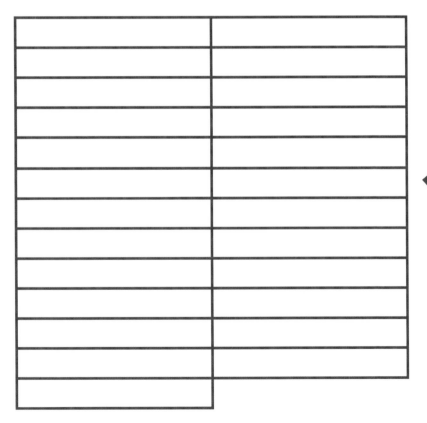

Great! Even if you didn't come up with 25 people (that's a *lot*), there are a ton of people who mean a great deal to you. But . . . do they *know* they are important to you?

Check out what Jesus tells His disciples in John 13:34-35:

> *I give you a new command. Love one another. You must love one another, just as I have loved you. If you love one another, everyone will know you are my disciples.*

Wow. Not only should we show others we love them, Jesus wants us to show love in such a huge way that it points people back to Him!

Sometimes it's easy to think that in order for people to know and believe in Jesus they need to know more about Jesus and understand *everything* He taught and *everything* He said and *everything* He did—even the stuff that's sometimes hard for adults to understand.

But what if it was more simple than all that? What if we simply chose to love others the way Jesus loves us?

You know . . .

Put others first.

Sacrifice what we want for what others want.

Forgive people who hurt us.

Spend time with people who are hurting.

Love everyone—even our enemies. (That means not just sticking to this list.)

When you **stand up** for things like that, you can't help but *stand out* from the crowd.

And when you stand out from the crowd, people will notice you. They'll watch you and wonder what makes you different. And when that happens, you simply say, "Jesus. I believe in Jesus, and that changes everything. He loves me, and He loves you. So I want to show His love to you."

People will see Jesus by how you love others.

So . . . how *can* you love others? There are all sorts of ways (that don't include flowers and chocolates). From little things like writing a note to big things like helping stock a food pantry for the homeless.

In fact, let's end today the way we started . . . with a timer set to three minutes. **Except this time, why don't you see if you can come up with 25 ways to show love to others? WRITE THEM OUT ON THE NEXT PAGE.**

Timer set? Ready? GO!

Now, use these charts to put love into practice by actually doing the things you wrote down. You can start with showing love to the people you already love. Then, try to branch out and show love to . . . *everyone*! Keep coming back to this page and check off the ideas you complete. **SEE IF YOU CAN COMPLETE ALL YOUR IDEAS BEFORE YOU FINISH THIS BOOK!**

DAY 5
MATTHEW 5:14-16

Quick! Grab a flashlight and your Bible and head some place *really* dark. Outside . . . a closet . . . the bathroom!

(I'll wait) . . .

Are you there? Good!

Is it dark?

Aha! Trick question! The room might be dark, but you have a flashlight. Without that flashlight, you wouldn't be able to see too well, would you? But you're smart enough to turn on your flashlight so you can see . . . even in a place that's pitch black!

When you're in a dark place, you need a flashlight or at least the dim glow from your cell phone screen in order to see your way around.

Basically, *you need light*.

In the book of Matthew, the Bible tells us about a time when Jesus was on a mountainside with His followers. As He was talking to them, He told them a little something about light.

PUT THAT FLASHLIGHT TO WORK AND CHECK OUT MATTHEW 5:14.

Did you see that? *You* are the light of the world.

That means that without *you*, there are parts of the world that would be dark.

Think about the flashlight you're holding right now. How does the light work? It beams from the flashlight and shines all around so you can see. You can't really see the actual flashlight. Instead, you see whatever the light is pointing towards.

Jesus says *you* are that light. But just like the flashlight in your hands doesn't shine on the actual flashlight, when you shine, you don't shine on yourself. What do you think you shine on? What do you think you point to when you stand up for what's right? **I'll give you a hint—take a look at Matthew 5:16.**

When you stand for what's right, you shine a light on God. You make it possible for others to see how awesome God is.

This week, when you stand up, remember that people can get to know God because of your courage to stand up for what's right.

TAKE A MOMENT AND WRITE OUT A PRAYER ON THE NEXT PAGE. THANK GOD FOR INVITING YOU TO HELP HIM SHINE HIS LIGHT ON THE WORLD. ASK HIM TO GIVE YOU COURAGE TO STAND UP FOR WHAT'S RIGHT AND POINT PEOPLE BACK TO HIM.

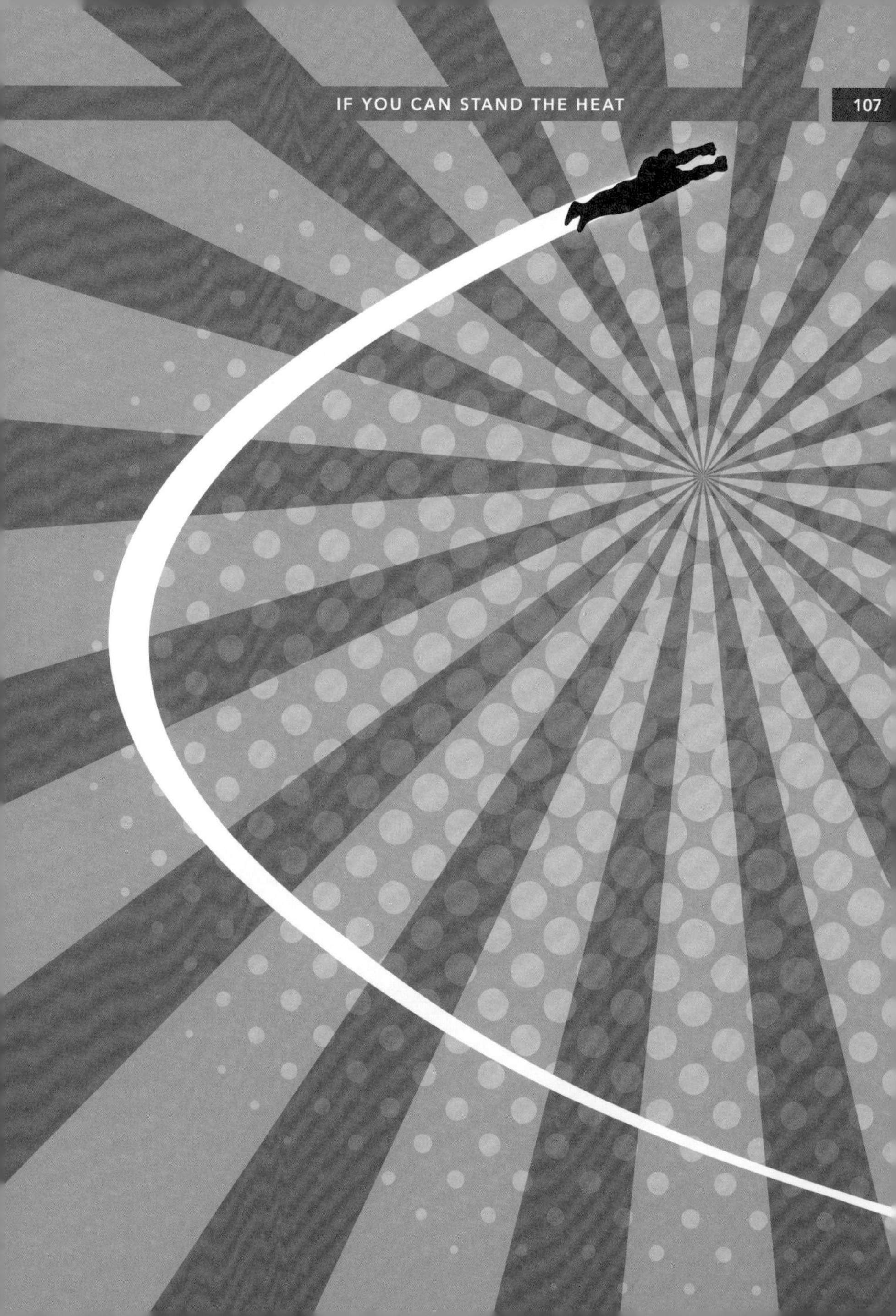

WEEKEND FOUR

You never know who's watching when you stand for what's right. (Not in a creeping-in-the-bushes kind of way.) When you stand for what's right, the people around you take note. And they wonder what gives you the courage and conviction to do the right thing. Maybe they start to see just how incredible God truly is.

Tyrel Wolfe was seven years old when he stuffed a very special shoebox full of toys and gifts to send halfway around the world. Christmas was coming and Tyrel knew that even though he lived in one of the wealthiest countries in the world, the United States of America, there were millions of families in the world who didn't have the money to buy Christmas gifts for each other and their children. The idea of a kid waking up on Christmas morning without one single present was enough to make Tyrel stand up and brighten the Christmas of just one kid.

And so, in the midst of writing out a list of all the toys he hoped to get on Christmas morning, Tyrel took the time to pick out small toys for a child in the Philippines—eight thousand miles from his home in Idaho. As he neatly arranged the toys he had chosen inside the shoebox, Tyrel tucked a picture of himself dressed as a cowboy with his name and address written on the back. He sealed the box and handed it off to the Operation Christmas Child program started by Samaritan's Purse. Perhaps Tyrel went on with his Christmas festivities without another thought about the small shoebox. But most likely, Tyrel spent his holidays wondering about the one child who received his thoughtful box of what he believed were the best toys a kid could hope for on Christmas morning.

Most likely, Tyrel thought about the journey his shoebox would take and what child would be waiting at the other end for it.

In just a few short weeks, Tyrel's box travelled to the other side of the world to a suburb of Manila in the Philippines where an eight-year-old girl named Joana received the shoebox during a Vacation Bible School graduation ceremony. Joana was so touched by the gift and the presentation that she made the decision to follow Jesus and live her life for God. Not long after, Joana's father made the same decision and became a pastor in their small town!

Joana loved the gifts Tyrel had packed for her. But above anything else in the box, she cherished the small photo of a blonde-haired boy in a cowboy shirt holding a lariat. Joana wrote a letter to the address on the back of the photo thanking Tyrel for the gift and explaining how much the small shoebox had impacted her life.

However, Joana never heard back from Tyrel. For some reason, her letter never made it to Idaho.

Time passed. Tyrel grew from a kid in second grade into a high school graduate. Joana was now nineteen years old and continuing to follow Jesus. And even though eleven years had passed, Joana never forgot the small shoebox that changed the direction of her entire life. Joana kept the small photo and thought of the blonde-haired kid from Idaho often. So one November morning, Joana decided to search for "Tyrel Wolfe" on Facebook. Dozens of profiles popped up but one stood out. There was one Tyrel Wolfe, location: Idaho. Could it be the same Tyrel Wolfe who had sent her the shoebox over a decade earlier?

Joana decided to take a chance and send a message to this Tyrel Wolfe from Idaho.

In the rural community of Midvale, Idaho, Tyrel checked his Facebook account before going to bed for the night. He was intrigued to find a message from a girl in the Philippines. He was even more shocked when he read the message thanking him for the shoebox he had so carefully filled as a seven-year-old kid. He had all but forgotten about that shoebox, but when he read the message from Joana, it all came flooding back. The toys, the self-addressed photo, the feeling he'd had knowing he had brightened another child's Christmas. However, as Tyrel read Joana's message, he realized he had done more than brighten her Christmas. His small box had helped change the direction of Joana's entire life!

Tyrel immediately responded to Joana and over the next year, Tyrel and Joana formed a friendship through photos and letters exchanged across the world. A couple of years after the beginning of their Facebook friendship, Tyrel found himself on a 24-hour flight to meet Joana in Manila! Tyrel spent ten days with Joana and her family. Later that year, Tyrel went back to the Philippines for an entire month. During this trip, Tyrel asked Joana's dad if he could marry her!

Joana and Tyrel are now happily married and living in Idaho near Tyrel's family. "I remember as a little boy, I was so excited to know the toys and other items I put in the box would bring joy to another child somewhere else in the world," Tyrel says. "I just didn't know the joy it would bring back to me one day."

Okay, so this isn't a typical story! Chances are, if you pack an Operation Christmas Child shoebox, you won't marry the kid you send it to. But this story is typical in one way: Tyrel's shoebox made a big difference in Joana's life! Not just because she got some cool toys she wouldn't have gotten otherwise. And not just because she met and married Tyrel. The box led Joana—and her dad—to follow Jesus. Because Tyrel stood up and sent a very special Christmas gift, Joana has a relationship with God and will spend eternity with Him. Now that is really cool!

WHEN YOU STAND FOR WHAT'S RIGHT, OTHERS CAN SEE GOD.

WEEK 5

SWEET DREAMS

(ARE MADE OF TREES)

DANIEL AND THE TREE DREAM
DANIEL 4

King Nebuchadnezzar of Babylon was one of the most powerful men on earth. With Daniel as one of his trusted advisors, the king had learned about the one true God, and even honored Him sometimes . . . when he felt like it. But mostly, King Nebuchadnezzar just honored himself. After all, when you're the most powerful man on earth, it's hard to believe anyone is cooler or more powerful than you . . . including this "one true God" Daniel went on and on about and served so faithfully.

But one day, as had happened years before, King Nebuchadnezzar had a frightening dream. He rang a bell, waking his servants from deep sleep. "Call my wise men," he commanded. "I must know what it means!"

The king explained the dream to his advisors, but he might as well have been speaking a foreign language. Not a single one of them could tell him what it meant. "Maybe it just means you shouldn't eat bratwurst with mustard before bed?" one of them dared to suggest. (You'd think King Nebuchadnezzar would have learned to call on Daniel first by now.)

"Oh, zither strings!" the king pouted. He paced the floor and finally sat back down, thumping the arms of his royal throne. "I want Daniel. Where's Daniel? He'll tell me what it means!"

Daniel wasn't home when the message arrived. When he finally returned and discovered the king's request, he hurried to the palace immediately and entered the throne room. "What is it, Your Majesty?" he asked.

"Finally!" cried the king and waved his hands toward the other advisors. "None of these fools can tell me what my dream means," he groused. The other advisors shrank back in humiliation and fear. "But I know your God is with you. *No mystery is too hard for you to figure out!*"

Daniel swallowed hard. The king's request was a difficult one, but Daniel spoke with God every day, and he knew that God would help him. "With God's help, I'll tell you what your dream means," Daniel told the king.

The king settled back on his throne and closed his eyes, trying to remember every detail. "In my dream," he began slowly, "I looked up and saw a beautiful, strong tree that reached up to touch the sky. The whole earth could see it! It gave food and shelter to every creature."

The king's eyes flashed wide as he recalled how the tone of the dream changed. "But then I saw a messenger from heaven. He ordered, '*Cut the tree down. Break off its branches. Strip off its leaves. Scatter its fruit. Let the animals under it run away. Let the birds in its branches fly off. But leave the stump with its roots in the ground.*'"

WITH GOD'S HELP, I'LL TELL YOU WHAT YOUR DREAM MEANS

The king frowned as he remembered the rest. "Then the messenger said, '*Let King Nebuchadnezzar become wet with the dew of heaven. Let him live with the animals among the plants of the earth. Let him no longer have the mind of a man. Instead, let him be given the mind of an animal. Let him stay that way until seven periods of time pass by.'"*

Daniel listened to every word, troubled, praying silently to God. "Is that all?" he finally asked.

"No," the king shook his head. "At the end, the messenger said, *'The decision is announced . . . So all who are alive will know that the Most High God is King. He rules over all kingdoms on earth.'"* King Nebuchadnezzar shivered as he begged, "Now, please. Tell me what it means!"

God had revealed the meaning of the dream to Daniel. But it wasn't good news for the king, who could see the truth in Daniel's face. *"Don't let the dream or its meaning make you afraid,"* the king told him.

"My king," Daniel began. He struggled for words, though he knew what he must say. "I wish the dream were about someone else! That big, strong tree that you saw? My king, that's you! *You* have become great and strong! And just like the tree's big branches, your rule has stretched out over the earth."

The king smiled and sat a little taller, flattered. Surely this wouldn't be so bad. But Daniel wasn't finished. He cleared his throat and continued.

"But my king, you don't honor the one true God. He has given an order that you will be driven away from people and live like a wild animal for seven periods of time. Then you will know it is God who truly rules over everything."

A wave of shock and surprise swept through the advisors lining the walls of the throne room. The king turned beet red, leaping from his throne. "Driven out of my very own land?!" he roared with infuriated disbelief.

"Wait!" Daniel jumped in. "The messenger gave a command to leave the stump and roots. So that means your kingdom will be returned to you when you recognize that God reigns over all."

The king settled back into his throne, shooting a glare at his advisors as if warning them to keep silent. His knuckles turned white as he gripped the arms of the throne. "Isn't there anything I can do to keep this from happening?"

"Please, please take my advice," Daniel begged. "Give up the wrong things you've done and do what is right! Be kind to people who aren't being treated well. Then, maybe things will go well for you."

PLEASE, PLEASE TAKE MY ADVICE

The king listened but soon forgot Daniel's wise words. He was too busy strutting around the city displaying his own power and wealth to stand up for what was right or show kindness to those in need. About a year later, he stood on the high roof of his palace, gazing out over Babylon. "Just look at this amazing city I've built with my mighty power to show how incredible I am!"

Immediately, a voice called out from heaven. *"King Nebuchadnezzar . . . Your royal authority has been taken from you. You will be driven away from people. You will live with the wild animals. . . . Seven periods of time will pass by for you. Then you will recognize that the Most High God rules over all kingdoms on earth."*

"What?" scoffed Nebuchadnezzar. "I'm the king. That's ridicu— ridi—" His voice began to fail him, turning into a wild roar. "Dridi— drrrrr— rrrrrrawr!" His eyes turned wild as he felt his ability to speak quickly slipping away. He clawed at his throat, but the words wouldn't come. In a few more moments, the king's mind grew cloudy. He didn't know who he was or how to act. Within a short time, he was out in the fields, scrabbling on his hands and knees, tearing out handfuls of grass to eat! His people and advisors stood at a distance, staring at their king in fascinated horror.

I PRAISE THE MOST HIGH GOD WHO LIVES FOREVER AND EVER!

Every day, dew soaked King Nebuchadnezzar. And just like God had said, for seven stretches of time, the king lived in the fields while his hair grew long and wild— like eagle's feathers. His fingernails grew so long it looked as if he had bird claws.

But at the end of it all, King Nebuchadnezzar finally looked up toward heaven. At long last, his mind cleared. He stared down in amazement at his shaggy unwashed self, the memory of who he was and what had happened slowly returning. Finally, he recovered his voice and found the words to speak. "I praise the Most High God who lives forever and ever! *His rule will last forever. His kingdom will never end. . . . He does as he pleases . . . . No one can hold back his hand.*"

Even though Nebuchadnezzar had lived like a wild animal for so long, his kingdom was restored back to him. Even his advisors returned to him. Occasionally they wanted to laugh when they recalled what he had looked like and how he had acted for so long—but none of them dared to do it.

In the end, King Nebuchadnezzar became even more powerful than he had been before. But this time, he didn't keep the honor for himself. *"Now I, Nebuchadnezzar, give praise and honor and glory to the King of heaven. Everything he does is right. All his ways are fair. He is able to bring down those who live proudly."*

King Nebuchadnezzar had learned once again to stand up for the one true God. But he might have learned without such a painful lesson if he had listened to Daniel's wise words the first time.

IF YOU WANT TO STAND FOR WHAT'S RIGHT, LISTEN TO SOMEONE WHO LISTENS TO GOD.

DAY 1
DANIEL 4

Have you ever heard God speak?

No, not audibly—not like a deep earth-quaking kind of voice from the sky . . . although people have heard God speak audibly. But, more often God speaks in other, more common and less terrifying ways *(aren't you glad?)*. He can speak to you when you read His Word, the Bible, by bringing certain words to life just for you. Or He can speak directly to your heart through thoughts since God's Holy Spirit lives inside of you.

Another awesome way that God speaks to us is through other people who know Him well—people who've been listening to God for a while. Those people learn wisdom from God. They start learning how to stand for what's right. And they can pass that wisdom on to you when you ask for it!

Think about it. When King Nebuchadnezzar asked Daniel—a man known to be in constant communication with God—for advice, Daniel was able to tell King Nebuchadnezzar exactly what God wanted him to do! **Just like King Nebuchadnezzar, it's important for you to seek out and surround yourself with people who are close to God. (And also, maybe take their advice when they give it.)**

Think through all the people you listen to, whether it's every day or just every so often. These people might be your teachers, coaches, neighbors, friends, parents or other family members. **WRITE DOWN THEIR NAMES HERE.**

Now, take a look at your list. Do any of these people listen to God? Maybe they talk about God a lot or pray and read their Bibles a lot. Maybe they actually gave you this book! Those are all good clues that someone is listening to God. **CIRCLE THE NAMES OF THE PEOPLE YOU THINK KNOW GOD AND TALK WITH HIM.**

This is a great list to keep in mind, because here's the thing: **If you want to stand for what's right, listen to others who listen to God.** So next time you're struggling with knowing what to do, find one of these people, share your problem . . . and start listening!

DAY 2
PROVERBS 1:5

So what do you think a wise person looks like? **GRAB SOME CRAYONS OR MARKERS AND DRAW ON THE FACE BELOW TO MAKE THE MOST WISE-LOOKING PERSON YOU CAN!**

Truth is, any one can be wise . . . the same way that anyone can be foolish! Wisdom doesn't depend on what you look like, but on the choices you make. Take a look at this verse from Proverbs—it's Proverbs chapter one, verse five:

Let wise people listen and add to what they have learned. Let those who understand what is right get guidance.

That may be a little confusing when you first hear it. So let's break it down. The verse is basically telling us two things about wise people:

1. They're always learning new things, even if they already know a lot.

2. They ask for help and direction when they need it. (Think about your dad on your last family road trip.)

It takes wisdom to know what's right. So if you want to stand for the right things, wise people can help you understand what's right in the first place.

Remember those people you wrote down yesterday? The ones who listen to God? If they've spent time learning from and asking God for help, that makes them wise—and it also makes them people you definitely want to go to when you've got questions.

WRITE DOWN THREE QUESTIONS YOU HAVE RIGHT NOW ABOUT LIFE OR ABOUT FAITH. It might be a hard situation you're in, or something one of your friends is facing. It might be a question about God or about following Him—or anything else you've been thinking about a lot lately.

1.

2.

3.

THIS WEEK, FIND ONE OF THOSE WISE PEOPLE YOU LISTED YESTERDAY AND ASK THEM YOUR QUESTIONS. AND LIKE THE VERSE SAYS, GET READY TO "ADD TO WHAT YOU'VE LEARNED!"

DAY 3
PSALM 1:1-3

Who are the people you spend the most time with? What kinds of things do you do when you spend time together? Have you noticed that you've started doing something simply because your friends do it? It might be a game you've started playing, a website you visit or maybe you eat way more Doritos than you did a couple of years ago! THINK OF ONE THING YOU'VE STARTED DOING OR DOING MORE OF SINCE HANGING OUT WITH YOUR FRIENDS AND WRITE IT HERE:

When you hang out with someone a lot, you start picking up their habits—what they do and how they act. And if they stand for the right things, well, you start standing for the right things too!

Psalm 1:1-3 has some cool stuff to say about this. Take a look:

Blessed is the person who obeys the law of the LORD.
They don't follow the advice of evil people.
They don't make a habit of doing what sinners do.
They don't join those who make fun of the LORD and his law.
Instead, the law of the LORD gives them joy.
They think about his law day and night.
That kind of person is like a tree that is planted near a stream of water.
It always bears its fruit at the right time.
Its leaves don't dry up.
Everything godly people do turns out well

MATCH EACH BIBLE VERSE REFERENCE WITH WHAT IT'S GOT TO SAY ABOUT HANGING OUT WITH WISE PEOPLE.

NOW PICK UP YOUR BIBLE OR LAUNCH YOUR BIBLE APP AND LOOK UP THE FOLLOWING PROVERBS.

Proverbs 12:15 — One person sharpens another.

Proverbs 15:22 — Those who live wisely are kept safe.

Proverbs 28:26 — Walk with wise people and become wise.

Proverbs 13:20 — Plans fail without good advice.

Proverbs 27:17 — Those who are wise listen to advice.

The Bible has a ton to say about hanging out with the right sort of people, huh? So the bottom line is this: The people you hang out with make a huge difference in what you think and what you do. So if you want to know what to stand for, hang out with wise people.

You just might find that wisdom rubbing off on you!

Proverbs 12:15: Those who are wise listen to advice. Proverbs 15:22: Plans fail without good advice. Proverbs 28:26: Those who live wisely are kept safe. Proverbs 13:20: One person sharpens another. Proverbs 27:17: Walk with wise people and become wise.

DAY 4
MARK 1:4-8

The Bible is filled with stories of wise—and not-so-wise!—people. And some of them aren't what you'd expect. For instance, what would you think of a man who lives out in the fields and brush, who dresses in clothes made from the hair of camels, and who eats bugs and honey? Which category would you think this bug-eating nomad falls under?

☐ WISE   ☐ NOT WISE

Believe it or not, that guy was really wise!

GRAB A BIBLE AND READ ABOUT HIM IN MARK 1:4-8.

His name was John the Baptist and he was quite the guy. But what he wore and ate wasn't all that made him stand out.

John had an important message. He pointed people to Jesus and explained how much they needed Him. Because John did this, many people turned away from their sins—the wrong things they were doing. Because of John the Baptist, people were ready to listen to Jesus and follow Him!

We've talked all week about listening to and hanging out with wise people. But the most important thing you can do is to listen to people who point you to Jesus.

But now it's time to turn the tables. While you listen to a lot of people, did you know that there are people listening to you? It's true. Friends, family, maybe even older people in your life see a difference in you because you follow Jesus.

THINK ABOUT IT FOR A SECOND AND WRITE DOWN A FEW OF THOSE PEOPLE IN YOUR LIFE.

_____

_____

_____

_____

_____

Now think about what it is your life is saying to these people. Are they learning about who God is from what you say and do? Or are they hearing something different?

WRITE DOWN A FEW THINGS YOU THINK THEY MIGHT HAVE LEARNED FROM YOU.

_____

_____

_____

_____

_____

Are these things you want your friends and family to be hearing from you? Or do you want to add to or change what you say to them? Whatever it is, look for ways that you can point the people who listen to you straight to Jesus!

DAY 5
LUKE 2:41-52

You learn things all the time. Take a second and think about the last thing you learned.

It might've been how to make brownies. Maybe it was what happens when you mix up Mentos® and diet soda! WHATEVER YOU LEARNED, WRITE IT DOWN HERE.

How about another question? Do you remember where you learned that? IF YOU DO, WRITE THAT PLACE HERE.

If someone was to ask you where you go to learn, where's the first place that comes to mind? School, right? And that makes sense! School is important, sure, but you can learn all sorts of things in all sorts of places. Take a quick look at the list below and write down what you might learn in each of the following places.

School _____

Home _____

Art studio _____

Field _____

Church _____

Dojo _____

Dance studio _____

Grandma's house _____

You're learning all the time, in all kinds of different places. Did you know that even Jesus, God's Son, had to learn things while He was here on earth? It's true!

TAKE A LOOK AT LUKE 2:41-52 IN YOUR BIBLE OR BIBLE APP.

Jesus spent a lot of time learning. He probably studied God's Word at a special place near His home while He was growing up. And when He was in Jerusalem, He went straight to God's house, the Temple, where He knew He could learn even more about God—and about what God wanted Him to stand for.

So here's the thing: If you want to know what to stand for, spend time at places that'll help you discover them.

Church is a great place to start. But so is your small group. Or maybe your grandparents' house—if they know a lot about God. Or even the library, to read stories about people who stood for the right things.

Ready, set . . . GO LEARN AND START STANDING!

WEEKEND FIVE

We all have people around us who do and say things that tell us they're listening to God. Maybe it's a friend who's really involved at church. Maybe it's a parent who's always encouraging you to pray or a neighbor who's always reading the Bible. There are ways to recognize those people and God tells us how important it is to learn from them.

Denzel Washington Jr. is now a very famous actor but his life didn't start off so promising. Denzel was born in Mount Vernon, New York—a city about 20 minutes outside of New York City. His father was a pastor who worked two side jobs to support the family. His mother was a beautician and eventually bought her own beauty shop. Denzel grew up during the civil rights movement and his mother was close friends with Betty Shabazz, the wife of the well-known activist, Malcom X, who was killed when Denzel was eight.

When Denzel was about ten years old, the civil rights movement hit home in a new and even more powerful way. Denzel had always gone to a school for African Americans while all the white kids in his city went to a completely separate school. But in the mid 1960s, Denzel's school was one of the first to combine with the school for white kids during the movement to desegregate the two communities. Not long after, when Denzel was 14 years old, his mom and dad got a divorce and his dad moved away.

All these things, from the effects of the civil rights movement during his childhood to his parents' divorce when he was a teen, were enough to point Denzel in a bad direction. Other kids in his neighborhood were making very bad decisions. They were getting in fights, skipping school, even trying drugs. At one point, after his parents' divorce, Denzel started down a bad path. Like many kids around him, he started making bad decisions.

When Denzel started getting in frequent fights in school and around the neighborhood, his mother encouraged him to change the people he was hanging out with. His mom got Denzel involved in a place called the Boys and Girls Club. The Boys and Girls Club was a place Denzel could go after school. Instead of hanging around his neighborhood with some of the kids who encouraged Denzel to make bad choices, Denzel could go to the Boys and Girls Club and play basketball or hang out in the game room with older kids and young adults who were really great influences.

As soon as Denzel started going to the Boys and Girls Club, he met a guy named Billy Thomas. "He made each of us feel like we were something special," Denzel says of Billy. As a boy, Denzel quickly began imitating Billy. He walked like Billy, tried shooting foul shots like Billy, sat in his chair like Billy. Denzel even started treating others with respect the way Billy did.

From Billy at the Boys and Girls Club, Denzel went on to imitate the integrity he found in the owner of the barbershop where he worked. Mr. Coleman was "a strong individual and true to his word," Denzel remembers.

When Denzel graduated high school, he followed in the footsteps of some of his friends from the Boys and Girls Club and went to college, sending his school banner back to the Boys and Girls Club in Mount Vernon to hang with the school banners of all the other successful kids from the community. When school got hard and Denzel was near failing, he once again listened to the wise advice of a teacher who saw a talent in him for acting. He switched his major to drama and got a raving letter of recommendation from a professor to go to graduate school. In the letter, Denzel's professor wrote, "If you don't have the talent to nurture this young man, then don't accept him." Denzel wasn't sure he was as talented as the letter made him out to be, but he respected his professor and wanted to live up to this man's words.

And eventually, he did.

Denzel Washington worked hard to get where he is today. It didn't come easy. Nothing was handed to him. But to this day, he will tell you that if he hadn't decided to change the people he was hanging out with, his life would look very different. Denzel learned a lot from the wise people around him. According to the mega-famous, Academy Award winning actor, if he hadn't chosen to listen to and imitate wise people in his community, he would most likely be a criminal instead of the world-renown movie star he is today.

IF YOU WANT TO STAND FOR WHAT'S RIGHT, LISTEN TO SOMEONE WHO LISTENS TO GOD.

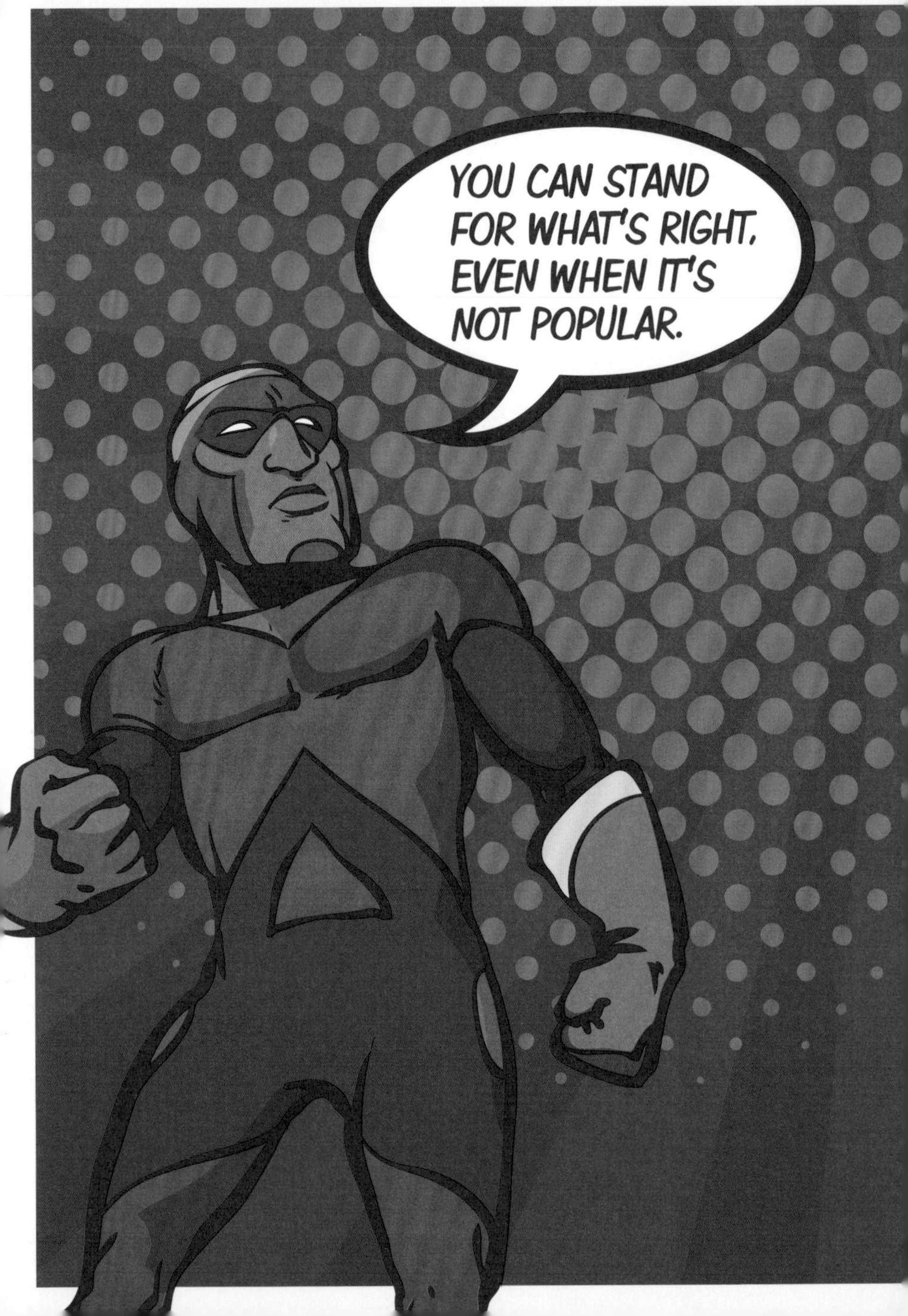
YOU CAN STAND FOR WHAT'S RIGHT, EVEN WHEN IT'S NOT POPULAR.

WEEK 6

WALL
SHOOK UP

HANDWRITING ON THE WALL
DANIEL 5

In the years when Daniel was captive in Babylon, kings rose and fell from power. And while King Nebuchadnezzar had sometimes acknowledged the one true God, one of the kings who came after him, King Belshazzar, most certainly did not.

"One true God?" he would scoff. "There are all kinds of gods. Dozens!"

King Belshazzar was proud and full of himself. So one day he threw a great party for one thousand of his nobles, and he basked in their abundant flattery and compliments.

"You have the largest army!"

"The tallest palace."

"The best hair!"

"A toast to the king!" one noble cried, lifting his cup.

King Belshazzar raised his cup to honor himself. But he noticed a tiny smudge; the cup just wasn't shiny enough. **"Hold it!" he commanded. "These cups aren't as magnificent as I am. Bring in those goblet thingies King Nebuchadnezzar took from Jerusalem!"**

Many years before when King Nebuchadnezzar had conquered Judah, he had stolen beautiful gold and silver cups from God's house in Jerusalem. They were goblets made to honor the one true God! Now the servants brought them out for Belshazzar's party.

The king surveyed his own glittering reflection in a golden cup. "Nice and shiny! Now we can really get this party started!"

The king and nobles toasted and drank from the cups, laughing and living it up for themselves and their false gods. "The gods will keep us safe from our enemies," laughed the king. "Here's to the god of war!"

The other nobles roared approval, drinking to all kinds of false gods. The party became even louder as the sun went down, and the king ordered lamps to be lit. **But in the midst of the chaos something incredible appeared in the light of the lampstand against the palace wall.**

The king stared, unable to believe what he was seeing. "It's . . . it's a hand!" he stammered.

NICE AND SHINY! NOW WE CAN REALLY GET THIS PARTY STARTED!

Sure enough, the fingers of a hand were tracing letters on the wall. But the hand wasn't attached to anything at all! The king's face turned white and his knees knocked together so hard that he collapsed into his chair. He blinked and squinted, but his eyes couldn't make any sense of the words. "What do they say?" he cried out. "Send for my wise men to tell me what it says!"

Servants woke all of Belshazzar's wise men, and they straggled in with their robes in disarray, rubbing their eyes and yawning.

"Read this writing and tell me what it means," King Belshazzar demanded. "If any one of you can do it, I'll make you the third highest ruler in the kingdom!"

But none of the so-called wise men could read the writing on the wall.

At the same time, some nobles tried to sneak close to see the writing, while others shoved against them, trying to get far away. The party was quickly turning to panic. However, one person at court—the queen mother—still remembered Daniel. She used her jeweled walking stick to beat a path to the front of the dining hall and raised her voice over the chaos.

"King Belshazzar, may you live forever!" she said. "Don't be afraid! Don't look so pale! I know a man in your kingdom who has the spirit of the holy gods in him. He has understanding and wisdom and good sense just like the gods. He was chief of those who tried to figure things out by using magic. And he was in charge of those who studied the heavens. Your father, King Nebuchadnezzar, appointed him to that position. King Nebuchadnezzar did this because he saw what the man could do. This man's name is Daniel. . . . Send for him. He'll tell you what the writing means."

The other advisors frowned, but the king was desperate. "Bring me this Daniel!" he ordered.

Daniel was brought to stand before King Belshazzar. He was an old man now, with white streaks in his hair and beard. But he still faithfully spent time with the one true God every single day. "You sent for me, King Belshazzar?" he asked.

"Read this writing and tell me what it means," the king commanded. "If you can, I'll make you third in command of the kingdom!"

Daniel gazed sadly at the proud king, who still held one of the shimmering holy cups from God's house. Daniel's eyes turned to all the nobles, who just wanted a quick answer so they could keep having a good time. Not a single person in the room really wanted to hear the hard truth.

"You can keep your gifts for yourself," Daniel said. "But I will read the writing for you. I'll tell you what it means."

"It says I'll live forever, right?" the king suggested, hopeful.

Daniel shook his head and looked the powerful king directly in the face. "King Belshazzar, the one true God was good to King Nebuchadnezzar. God made him the most powerful person in the world. But the king became very proud. So God took him from the throne and made him like a wild animal, until Nebuchadnezzar recognized that God rules over all."

BRING ME THIS DANIEL!

The king's fingers tapped impatiently against the arms of his chair; he didn't like where this was going. "Yeah, yeah. Enough with the backstory."

Daniel took a deep breath. Belshazzar wasn't going to be happy with the truth—especially in the middle of a party. And he had the power to punish Daniel in any way he chose. **"You knew all of this, King Belshazzar," Daniel pointed out. "But you haven't paid attention. You are still prideful. You've mocked the one true God. You've drank from cups taken from His house, while praising false gods who can't see or hear anything."**

Belshazzar narrowed his eyes in anger. But Daniel kept right on going. "You didn't honor God. He holds in his hand your very life and everything you do. So he sent the hand that wrote on the wall. Here is what was written: 'MENE, MENE, TEKEL, PARSIN.'"

"Yeah, okay, that's still Greek to me!" groused the king.

Daniel continued with a translation. "'Mene' means that God has put a limit on the amount of time that you're going to be king. You're not going to be king for much longer."

Everyone in the room gasped. Those were dangerous words. They could get Daniel in big trouble!

But Daniel didn't stop. "'Tekel' means that God has put you on a scale to see if you measure up, and you don't. 'Parsin' means that God is going to take away your authority as king. He is going to give it to the Medes and Persians."

When Daniel finished with the terrible news, the entire room was deadly silent. He braced himself: Belshazzar could order him killed immediately.

But instead, the king seemed determined to put a good face on the terrible news. **After a long moment, he plastered a smile on his still pale face and chuckled. "Well . . . ha, ha! There you have it. Congrats, Daniel. Third highest ruler in the land! Bring him purple clothes! And a gold chain!"**

Sad and weary, Daniel allowed King Belshazzar to honor him. He knew the party couldn't last. That very night, Belshazzar's enemies, the Medes and Persians, conquered Babylon and killed the king. Darius the Mede became the new King of Babylon in his place, just as the writing on the wall had foretold.

DAY 1
DANIEL 5

What would you do if you were at a sleepover with your friends and a hand appeared out of nowhere and started writing on the wall? Would you start screaming hysterically? Would you run in circles around the room? Would you hide under fifteen sleeping bags?

DRAW YOUR REACTION HERE:

Well, that's pretty much what happened to King Belshazzar. You can read the whole story in Daniel 5. *(And if the same thing happens to you, you might want to consider drinking out of different cups. Just sayin'.)*

So King Belshazzar is hosting a party to end all parties. A thousand of his nobles show up and he tries to impress everyone by bringing out the goblets King Nebuchadnezzar had stolen from Judah way back when he marched Daniel and his friends out of their homes to Babylon. The goblets were special. They had been used in the Temple to worship God. But King Belshazzar and his buddies start drinking from them and praising their false gods.

But that whole drinking-from-the-holy-grail thing never goes over well. And as soon as King Belshazzar does it, this floating hand appears and writes an encrypted message on the wall.

Makes you wonder if everyone went crazy. Screaming. Scrambling to get away. Running in circles. Crying and waving their arms. They might have looked a lot like the picture you drew a minute ago.

And, as it turns out (*again*) Daniel is the only person in the kingdom who can decipher the message (with God's help) for the king.

The problem was, when Daniel saw what the message said, he realized the message wasn't anything good. Which is usually the case when a floating hand scribbles on the wall. But, it would have been a lot easier for Daniel to deliver a message to the king that said something like, "Congrats on all the success! You deserve it!"

Daniel knew that if he shared what the writing said, it wasn't going to be a popular message. He knew it would be so unpopular the king would have every right to kill Daniel on the spot for even saying the words!

Daniel had a choice. He could make something up, calm the king down and let the festivities continue. Or he could do what was right and tell Belshazzar the truth of God's message, even if it meant the king could get upset and take it out on Daniel.

Daniel ended up doing the right thing. And even though it was bad news for the king, the king made Daniel the third most important leader in the entire kingdom. God had Daniel's back and took care of the details.

Now, hopefully you'll never be put in a situation as dire as Daniel's. But there will be times when standing up for what's right means losing the popularity contest in a major way. You might be the bearer of bad news. You might be the one to bring the party to a screeching halt. But if you feel like you need to **stand up**, you can trust God to work out the details. He's got your back, too.

SO WHAT DO YOU NEED TO REMEMBER THIS WEEK? WELL, YOU'LL JUST HAVE TO CRACK THE CODE TO FIND OUT.

Here's a hint!
22 = E
09 = R

__ __ __|__ __ __|__ __ __ __ __|__ __ __|__ __ __ __ '__
02 12 06 24 26 13 08 07 26 13 23 21 12 09 04 19 26 07 08

__ __ __ __ __|__ __ __ __|__ __ __ __|__ __'__|__ __ __
09 18 20 19 07 22 05 22 13 04 19 22 13 18 07 08 13 12 07

__ __ __ __ __ __ __.
11 12 11 06 15 26 09

DAY 2
1 TIMOTHY 4:12

Remember back in the day when your preschool teacher asked you, "What do you want to be when you grow up?"

WHAT DID YOU SAY?

Did you want to be a fireman or policeman? How about an astronaut or superhero? Maybe a ballerina or princess?

How would you answer that question now? If you could be anyone or anything, who would you choose to be and why? Write down some thoughts below.

_____

_____

_____

_____

Sometimes you might see famous people on TV or in a movie and wish you were like them and could do all the things they get to do because they're rich, popular and important. Maybe you've wished you were old enough to do all those important things.

There's a pastor from the early church who might have thought the same sort of thing—that he was too young to make a real difference. His name was Timothy. He was a young pastor a long, long time ago, back when people first started to follow Jesus.

But a guy named Paul, who was also a pastor and a mentor to Timothy, wrote Timothy a letter encouraging him. We know this because Paul's letter to Timothy makes up the book of 1 Timothy in our Bibles today.

SO GRAB A BIBLE OR BIBLE APP AND READ 1 TIMOTHY 4:12.

Pretty cool, huh?

Paul is basically telling Timothy, "Don't wait until you're older to begin doing all that God made you to do."

And the same thing applies to you today! You don't have to wait until you're old enough to make a difference. You can make a difference now! Today! You can stand up for what's right whether you're five or 95! You don't have to wait until you're older to show conviction. So, how about another question?

When people talk about you now, what do you want them to say about you? What do you want to be known for right now? **JOT DOWN A FEW IDEAS BELOW.**

_____

_____

_____

_____

That's great! Now, make it happen. You don't have to wait to stand up for what's right. Start setting an example for those who are older than you. Show them what God can do through kids just like you!

DAY 3
ACTS 12:1-18

Let's start today off with a little fun challenge. Try escaping from this maze.

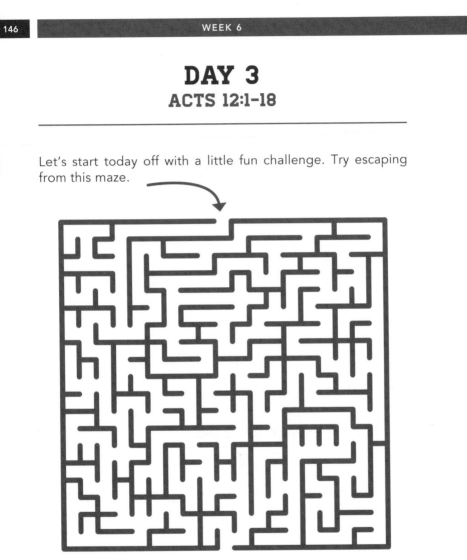

Maybe you saw that maze and it freaked you out. You just knew that you'd end up trapped in there with no way to escape.

Or maybe you took a look at it and immediately said, "I've got this."

But even if you were able to escape (and I hope you were!), you've got to admit that maze was pretty tricky, right?

Back in the book of Acts, Peter found himself trapped in jail with no way to escape. Well . . . no humanly possible way to escape.

YOU CAN READ THE WHOLE STORY IN ACTS 12:1–18.

*(And you should—this story is **epic**.)*

Here's the lowdown on what happened . . .

Peter was thrown into prison for talking about Jesus. But he wasn't just thrown into some old jail cell and left alone. Nope. There were 16 soldiers standing guard just to make sure Peter didn't escape.

(Wow. They really didn't want people talking about Jesus.)

But while Peter was in prison, the *whole church* was praying for him! Seriously!

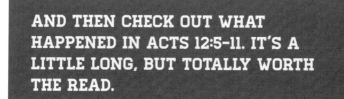

AND THEN CHECK OUT WHAT HAPPENED IN ACTS 12:5–11. IT'S A LITTLE LONG, BUT TOTALLY WORTH THE READ.

So go ahead, get to reading!

Whoa! Pretty powerful prayer, right?

Peter was trapped. He knew that staying in prison could mean he would be killed. He had no way to escape. But he had something better. He had a whole bunch of people praying for him.

God sent an angel to help Peter escape by walking right out of the jail—with guards all around and everything! That's the power of prayer. When we pray, God can do the impossible.

See, **when you stand up, God shows up**.

When you **stand up**, you might feel scared that you'll lose friends or feel like you're the only one standing for what's right. But when you feel scared or trapped, the first thing you should do is pray.

And when you pray, God will show up. It might not be exactly how you expect—Peter could never have guessed that an *angel* would show up in prison—**but God will show up when you stand up for what's right and show conviction.**

DAY 4
MARK 8:34-38

There's this show on TV called *The Price Is Right*. You might've heard of it, but it's probably on while you're in school. It's a game show and the basic idea of the game is that contestants guess how much things cost. And if they can guess correctly, they win whatever that thing is—even a *new car*!

Sound like the kind of game show you could totally *rock*? Let's test out your pricing skills with this matching game. **DRAW A LINE BETWEEN THE ITEM AND ITS DOLLAR AMOUNT. WHAT'S THE *AVERAGE PRICE* OF THE FOLLOWING . . .**

A regular-sized candy bar	**$5,000.00**
A 12 oz. can of soda	**$85.00**
A trip for four to Disney	**$635**
A moped scooter	**$1.25**
A pair of basketball sneakers	**$6,500.00**
A new laptop	**$1.00**

No matter where you go, it seems like everything has a cost—even if the cost has nothing to do with money.

Take homework for example. Doing your homework is important, right? But it does cost you something—like playing less video games or not playing outside with friends.

ANSWERS: Candy Bar - $1.25, Soda - $1.00, Disney - $5,000, scooter - $6,500, Sneakers - $85, Laptop - $635

Sure, we usually think of "cost" in terms of actual money. But what about these things? What will they "cost" you (other than money)?

Joining a sports team or a dance company?

Eating donuts every meal for a month?

Following Jesus and standing up for what's right?

Everything costs something—including following Jesus and standing up for what's right.

GRAB YOUR BIBLE OR BIBLE APP AND FIND MARK 8. TAKE A MINUTE TO READ VERSES 34 AND 35.

Grab your Bible or Bible app and find Mark 8. Take a minute to read verses 34 and 35.

Got it? Great!

Those verses might have been a bit hard to understand, but they mean something like this: Lots of people were starting to follow Jesus. And Jesus wanted them to know what following

Him was all about. Jesus really doesn't hold anything back. He basically says,

"Following Me is gonna cost you everything."

Sounds pretty scary, huh? But, Jesus says when you give up everything for Him and let go of what you want for what He wants, you actually *gain* everything.

This doesn't mean you'll be rich and famous. It also doesn't mean that standing up will be easy. But it will mean that you can have . . .

peace when life gets hard,

comfort when you're upset,

love when you feel alone . . .

. . . because God will always be with you.

Standing up will cost you something, but that doesn't mean you don't do it. I think you can take Jesus's word for it and know that when you follow Jesus and **stand up** for what He wants, it'll be worth it!

DAY 5
MATTHEW 16:13-20

People are known for all sorts of things. **TAKE A MINUTE AND WRITE DOWN WHAT EACH OF THESE PEOPLE ARE KNOWN FOR.** (And don't worry—you can ask for help if you're not so sure!)

Martin Luther King Jr. _____

Babe Ruth _____

Dr. Seuss _____

Albert Einstein _____

Vincent Van Gogh _____

Beethoven _____

Amelia Earhart _____

One day, the book of Matthew tells of a time when Jesus asked His disciples what He was known for. "Who do the people say that I am?" He asked them.

His disciples gave several answers. They told Him that some people thought Jesus might actually be John the Baptist. Others thought He might be one of the prophets from hundreds of years ago who had come back to life.

But Jesus had a follow-up question, one that got a bit more personal. Matthew 16:15 says that Jesus asked His disciples,

"But what about you? . . . Who do you say I am?"

What do you think they said? The Bible doesn't tell us what most of the disciples said or what any of them were thinking.

But one person spoke up and answered: Peter. He knew exactly what to say.

"You are the Messiah. You are the Son of the Living God."

Now, here's the thing. To you and me this might not sound like such a big deal—*of course Jesus is the Messiah, the Savior!* Jesus is the Savior God promised since the beginning of time! But back then, not many people believed that. Many people thought Jesus was just a good teacher who did miracles and taught interesting things. But the Savior? The One who would rescue God's people? The One who God had promised since the beginning of time? God's own Son? That was a huge claim.

So it was a pretty big deal when Peter said that Jesus was the Messiah. Peter was recognizing Jesus for who He actually is. Not just a person, but God's very own Son. Not just a good teacher, but the Savior of all people from all time. By naming Jesus as the Savior, Peter was saying, "You—a simple-looking, scruffy carpenter's Son—are *the One* God sent to save us. And because of You, *everything will change.*"

Peter stood up for Jesus. But you have to realize that Peter had seen Jesus perform miracles. And Peter had heard Jesus preach incredible truths. Peter must have realized that Jesus was who He said He was. So when Jesus asked him the question, "Who do you say that I am?," Peter knew he could stand up and say, "You're the Savior!"

And you can, too. You may not have experienced everything that Peter did. You may not even know that much about

Jesus—but you can find out what Jesus said and did by reading through the Gospels: Matthew, Mark, Luke and John. These are the stories that Jesus' own friends and followers wrote down about His life.

You can also find out how Jesus is still doing incredible things today when you talk to people you know who've experienced Jesus' love first hand.

It's important to know and believe just who Jesus is and how incredible His life was. Because when you believe that Jesus is the Savior, you can stand up . . . for anything!

WEEKEND SIX

Standing for what's right isn't always the most popular thing to do. And sometimes, you're the first one—or maybe the only one—willing to stand up. Check out this true story about a girl named Malala and how she stood up for what was right even though it was really unpopular.

Malala Yousafzai was born in Pakistan in 1997. Growing up, Malala was unique in the fact that her father valued her education and encouraged her to go to school. **Most girls in Pakistan were discouraged or even forbidden from getting an education.** But Malala's father risked great danger by making sure Malala was educated and had all the opportunities her two brothers did. While Malala's father was making sure his daughter had an education, the local Taliban extremists were doing all they could to make sure Pakistani girls did not get an education.

When Malala was 11 years old, she began standing up and speaking to audiences about girls' rights to get an education. "How dare the Taliban take away my basic right to education?" Malala said to the press in 2008.

Malala wasn't just standing up against any old bully. Malala was standing up against *the Taliban*. All over the region, the Taliban was banning girls from going to school and forbidding women from leaving the house. The schools were segregated by gender and armed Taliban militants began standing guard outside the schools for girls, causing the girls' schools to shut down completely.

But that didn't stop Malala from doing what was right. She soon heard of a news station looking for a girl to write a blog, anonymously of course, about her experience trying to get an education under Taliban rule. Malala was glad for the opportunity to stand up and have her voice heard. She began handwriting blogs that she would secretly pass off to a reporter who would then scan and post them. Malala did all this under the false name, Gul Makai.

The Taliban became more and more aggressive, blowing up girls' school buildings and shooting rounds of artillery fire through the night to instill fear in Malala and her friends. But even though her school was shut down and the Taliban was threatening, Malala continued studying and writing.

Before long, the girls' schools opened again and Malala and her friends bravely entered the doors of one of the school buildings that was still standing. The schools were open for a short time but the fighting was not over.

As time passed, Malala's blog grew more and more popular and by the time she was 12 years old, her identity was revealed. She became the face of the movement against the Taliban's restrictive laws on girls and women. She wrote articles and made appearances on local as well as international news stations.

When she was 14, Archbishop Desmond Tutu nominated Malala for the International Children's Peace Prize. She was the first Pakistani girl to ever be nominated for the prize and the announcement read, "Malala dared to stand up for herself and other girls and used national and international media to let the world know girls should also have the right to go to school."

Two months later, Malala won Pakistan's first National Youth Peace Prize. A campus at the local college was opened for

women and a secondary school was named in honor of 14-year-old Malala. In the beginning of 2012, Malala began to organize the Malala Education Foundation, which would help poor girls go to school.

With all this attention and action being taken on Malala's behalf, it came as no surprise when she began receiving death threats from the Taliban. **Yikes!** She was only 14 years old and had already made a major change in her community by standing for what's right . . . but that also put an even bigger target on her back from the Taliban.

On October 9, 2012, a Taliban gunman got on the bus Malala was taking while coming home from an exam. "Which one of you is Malala?" the man demanded to know. Malala was identified and then shot in the head.

Miraculously, the Taliban's assassination attempt didn't work! Malala survived! After traveling to the very best hospitals in Europe and receiving the best care there was to offer, Malala fully recovered by March of 2013.

Instead of silencing Malala, the Taliban's assassination attempt made her even more famous and got all kinds of international attention. Numerous celebrities and even President Obama spoke out against the attack on Malala. **She was only 16 years old and had become a worldwide activist, holding meetings with Queen Elizabeth at Buckingham Palace and Barack Obama in Washington D.C. She even spoke to the United Nations as well as Harvard University.**

And when Malala Yousafzai was only 17 years old, she became the youngest recipient of the Nobel Peace Prize for her struggle against the suppression of children.

Malala stood up for what was right in a *big* way. What was right was not popular and it definitely cost her a lot to show conviction but none of that stopped her from doing what she knew was right.

YOU CAN STAND FOR WHAT'S RIGHT EVEN WHEN IT'S NOT POPULAR.

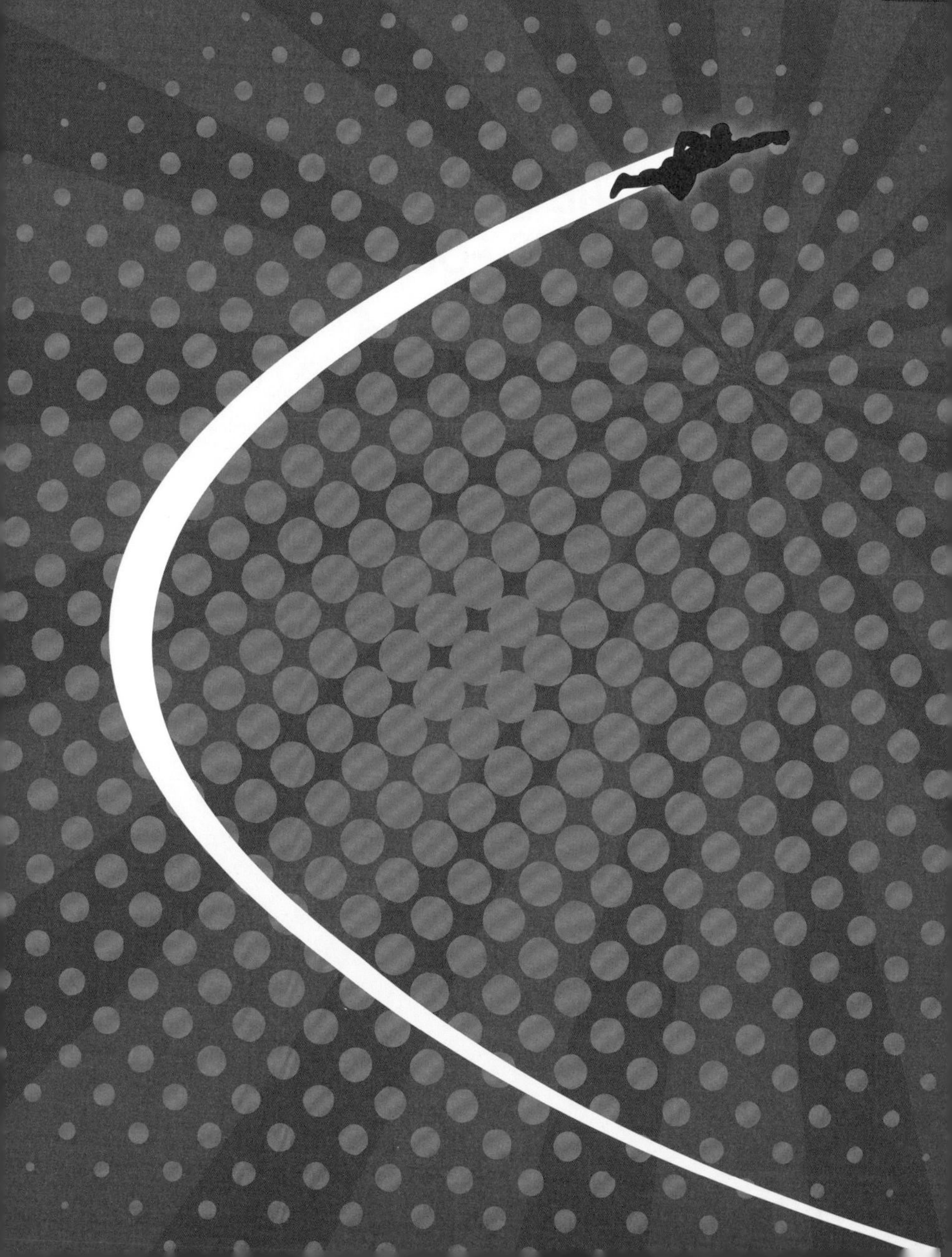

WEEK 7

I WALK THE LION

DANIEL AND THE LION'S DEN
DANIEL 6

When Darius became King of Babylon, he knew he needed help ruling the vast kingdom and controlling his great wealth. So one of his first orders of business was appointing 120 royal rulers to watch closely over the kingdom. And just to make sure those 120 royal rulers were doing their jobs, King Darius chose three *exceptional* leaders to be in charge of them. **Daniel was one of those three leaders.**

The other two leaders took every advantage of their new position, strutting and gleaming in the light of their new important title—second in command of the entire kingdom.

But when Daniel heard the news that he had been given such an important position, he went home to his upstairs room and, as always, prayed with his windows open since they faced the direction of Jerusalem, the capital of his homeland. "God, thank You for giving me this position," he began. "Please help me to serve the king and the people well. But most of all, help me to always serve You well."

As soon as he finished talking with God, Daniel began the difficult job of overseeing so many other leaders. **God was with him, and Daniel did well—so well that King Darius was impressed. Before long, King Darius decided to promote Daniel above the other two leaders.**

But when the other two leaders heard about the king's plan to put Daniel in charge of the kingdom, they were less than congratulatory. The two other leaders, along with the rest of the royal rulers, were jealous that Daniel might be promoted and looked for a way to bring him down. But they couldn't find one single itty bitty thing wrong with his work. Daniel was trustworthy. He worked diligently and honorably. He didn't do anything against the law of the kingdom. In fact, all he seemed to do was work well and pray to his one true God. That's when the other leaders got an idea.

"If we're going to get rid of Daniel, we're going to have to do it by making it illegal to follow his God."

The two leaders and the royal rulers cooked up a terrible plan and took it directly to the king.

"King Darius, may you live forever!" they flattered him. "You're so awesome, we think you should give an order. For the next 30 days, no one can pray to anyone but you."

"Fascinating," the king noted. "But what happens if someone breaks this rule?

GOD, THANK YOU FOR GIVING ME THIS POSITION

"Oh, just a little trip to the lions' den," they told him quickly. "All you have to do is make it a law. As soon as it's written down in the laws of the Medes and Persians, everyone in the kingdom has to obey. No take backs!"

It was true: once an order was written down as a law, no one could change it. Not even the person who made it!

But Darius was so flattered he didn't think twice about creating the new law. "I'm a good king!" he told himself. "Why shouldn't the people pray to only me? I'll do it!"

Daniel heard about the law immediately, but nothing could stop him from his daily habit of praying to the one true God. Just as he did every day, he prayed with his windows open toward Jerusalem. **"Dear God, thank You for giving me everything I need. Please help me to stand for You, no matter what."**

The other leaders were hiding nearby, watching. "Ha ha!" one of them cackled with glee. "I can see his bushy grey beard at the window. He's praying!"

Gleeful, the other leaders raced to find King Darius. "Didn't you sign a law—" the first said breathlessly as the others cut in, all trying to be first.

"A law that says no one can pray to any god but you—"

"—For 30 whole days—"

"—Or they get thrown into a den of lions?"

"Calm down!" commanded the king. "Of course I did. Just the other day."

"Well, Daniel's already broken your law," the leaders announced triumphantly.

"He *what*?" The king's eyes popped open wide. "Daniel?!"

The leaders smirked. "Daniel prays to his God three times a day!"

King Darius was terribly upset by how he had been tricked. Daniel was his most trusted advisor, and the king didn't want him to be hurt. But official laws were so strong that even the king couldn't find a way out. At sunset, Daniel was brought out and lowered into the lions' den!

"You always serve your God faithfully," King Darius called out. *"So may he save you!"*

Immediately, a heavy stone was placed over the mouth of the den. In the dark, Daniel continued praying. **"God, thank You for helping me stand up for You. I trust that You will take care of me, even here!"**

King Darius returned to his palace, a sinking feeling in the pit of his stomach. He couldn't choke down any food or close his eyes for even a moment. All night, he paced the rooftop gardens, staring through the darkness toward the place where the lions were kept.

As the sun finally rose, Darius rushed to the lions' den. "Remove the stone this instant!" he ordered.

Darius peered into the pit. His eyes, blinded by the sun, could see only gloom. "*Daniel! You serve the living God. You always serve him faithfully. So has he been able to save you from the lions?*"

For a moment, the king heard nothing more than a deep, rumbling purr. **Then Daniel emerged into the light—unharmed!**

"*Your Majesty, may you live forever!*" Daniel said. "*My God sent his angel. And his angel shut the mouths of the lions. They haven't hurt me at all. That's because I haven't done anything wrong in God's sight. I've never done anything wrong to you either, Your Majesty.*"

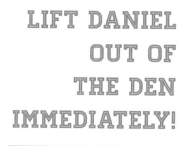

LIFT DANIEL OUT OF THE DEN IMMEDIATELY!

"Lift Daniel out of the den immediately!" Darius commanded.

Darius was overjoyed to see Daniel safe. But his anger burned against the men who had tricked him into signing the terrible law. "Those fools. Bring them here at once!" he told his guards. "Throw *them* in the lions' den!"

The men who had tried to destroy Daniel lost their own lives instead. And King Darius immediately sent for his scribe to write a letter to all of the people in the land. "Say this:" the king instructed. "'*I order people in every part of my kingdom to respect and honor Daniel's God. He is the living God. He will live forever. His kingdom will not be destroyed. . . . He has saved Daniel from the power of the lions.*'"

God gave Daniel success all through the reign of King Darius. And Daniel continued to stand for the one true God.

DAY 1
DANIEL 6

When you hear the word "habit," what comes to mind?

Biting your nails?
Chewing on your pencil?
Picking your nose?

It's true. When we think about habits, all the bad ones come to mind first. But there are people who have actually developed some good habits that help them work harder, play stronger and even live better lives!

Think about professional athletes. They eat well, get rest, drink lots of water and regularly train with coaches. On top of that, some sports have really specific training habits.

SEE IF YOU CAN MATCH THE GOOD HABIT WITH THE SPORT. DRAW A LINE BETWEEN THE ONES THAT GO TOGETHER.

Basketball   corner kicks
Baseball   laps
Soccer   back handsprings
Tennis   serving
Swimming   free throws
Gymnastics   fielding grounders

And then there's Daniel. Throughout the past few weeks, you've seen how Daniel was able to **stand up** for what's right in all sorts of situations. From eating God-honoring foods to seeking God for dream interpretations and coded messages,

Daniel was constantly standing up and doing the right thing in God's eyes. But he had never been tested the way he was when King Darius was forced to throw him in the lions' den. Sure, his life had been in danger before. At any moment in the past, one of the kings of Babylon could have decided they didn't like Daniel or his dedication to the one true God and ordered him to be killed. But never before had he looked death in the face . . . well, more accurately, looked a den of hungry lions in the face.

Daniel had been appointed as one of the king's three most elite rulers. Not only that, he was the king's favorite. Needless to say, that didn't make the other appointed rulers too happy. In fact, check out Daniel 6:4.

> *"So they looked for a reason to bring charges against Daniel. They tried to find something wrong with the way he ran the government. But they weren't able to. They couldn't find any fault with his work. He could always be trusted. He never did anything wrong. And he always did what he was supposed to."*

Can you imagine being the type of person who had such a great reputation that no one could find anything wrong with what you did? That was Daniel!

So the other leaders got creative. When King Darius' royal rulers convinced him to make a law commanding everyone in the Medo-Persian Empire to pray to him and *only him*, Daniel understood what the new law meant. He understood that by praying to and acknowledging the one true God, he was purchasing a one-way ticket to the lions' den.

But that didn't stop Daniel from doing what he knew was right. Check out what Daniel did when he heard about the new law in Daniel 6:10.

"Daniel found out that the king had signed the order. In spite of that, he did just as he had always done before. He went home to his upstairs room. Its windows opened toward Jerusalem. He went to his room three times a day to pray. He got down on his knees and gave thanks to his God."

Daniel had a *habit* of worshipping God. **He knew that God could be trusted no matter what. So Daniel kept going to God in prayer. He knew he had to keep doing what was right even if he was caught and thrown into the lions' den.**

When they caught Daniel praying to God, King Darius had no choice but to throw him into the den. But God closed the lions' mouths! Daniel was saved!

Daniel lived in a place where most of the people didn't worship God. Yet Daniel stayed strong and prayed to God even when he knew he'd get in trouble. He was in the habit of standing for what's right, so when it came time to stand up in the face of something really scary (what's scarier than a hungry lion?!), all Daniel had to do was continue his habit.

You can get in the habit of standing for what's right too. You'll probably never face a hungry lion for doing what's right, but you may face other scary things for standing for what's right. That's why it's important to get in the habit of standing up now, so when the time comes, showing conviction will be the first thing you do.

So get prepared. **Daniel prayed every day. He knew God's Word. He had friends who helped him remember the right things to do.** Those are all things you can do right now!

Dare to live like Daniel. **Get in the habit of standing up for what's right.**

GET IN THE HABIT OF STANDING FOR WHAT'S RIGHT.

DAY 2
JAMES 1:22-24

First things first. Grab a dry erase marker and head to the bathroom. (Don't worry—no toilets will be involved.)

Are you there? Great. Now, take a good look at yourself in the mirror.

SMILE.
FROWN.
GET ANGRY.
MAKE THE HAPPIEST FACE YOU CAN IMAGINE.

You look good, don't you?

Now, take that dry erase marker . . . (You heard me say *dry erase*, right?)

Look at yourself in the mirror again. Only this time, **USE THE DRY ERASE MARKER AND DRAW ON THE MIRROR TO MAKE IT LOOK LIKE YOU HAVE A MUSTACHE OR CRAZY EYEBROWS LIKE YOUR GREAT UNCLE HOWARD. AND WHILE YOU'RE AT IT, GUVE YOURSELF SOME CRAZY HAIR TOO!**

How do you look? Pretty funny, right?

What would you do if you woke up tomorrow morning and actually looked like this (no marker or anything)?

Would you shrug it off and head out the door to school or would you comb your hair down and trim your eyebrows?

I'm guessing if you knew you looked *this* messy, you'd do something about it, right? Otherwise, you'd look pretty silly walking into school.

Jesus' brother, James, actually wrote a very similar example in the Bible (except he didn't mention your Great Uncle Howard).

GRAB YOUR BIBLE OR SEARCH YOUR BIBLE APP FOR JAMES 1:22-24.

"Don't just listen to the word. You fool yourselves if you do that. You must do what it says. Suppose someone listens to the word but doesn't do what it says. Then they are like a person who looks at their face in a mirror. After looking at themselves, they leave. And right away they forget what they look like."

Guess what "word" James is talking about? Yep, he's talking about God's Word, the Bible.

It's sorta like James is saying that God's Word is like a mirror. When you read it, it's gonna show you something about your life that you might want to change. Maybe you'll start to see that you . . .

. . . could be more generous.

. . . need to obey your parents.

. . . should stop complaining.

But if you don't change, it's just like seeing that you have a giant smear of chocolate sauce on your cheek and just leaving it there. Not very wise of you, huh?

James is saying that it doesn't mean much if you know something but don't follow through and do something about it.

More often than not, we know the right thing to do. We see something happen and feel like we should stand up for what's right. But how often do we take what we know is right and do it? When we feel like there's something we need to do, we should probably go ahead and do it, right?

Maybe all you need is a reminder. **TAKE THAT MARKER YOU USED EARLIER (THAT *DRY ERASE* ONE) AND WRITE YOURSELF A NOTE ON THE MIRROR. THE NEXT TIME YOU LOOK AT YOURSELF, YOU'LL ALSO REMEMBER TO STAND UP FOR WHAT'S RIGHT.**

If you can't think of what to write, here are some phrases to get you started:

Just DO the right thing.

Trust God and stand up.

**Conviction isn't something you feel,
it's something you DO.**

What does God say I should DO?

Look for a way to stand up and DO it!

DAY 3
GALATIANS 6:9

How long can you hold your breath? **GIVE IT A SHOT—TIME YOURSELF.** Maybe compete against someone in your house or a friend next door.

How long could you do it?

That was pretty good. Do you think if you tried again, you could hold it for even longer? Maybe two minutes? Or three?? How about 22 minutes?!

That'd be crazy, right? Well, not for Stig Severson. He actually held his breath underwater for 22 minutes (and 22 seconds) straight! (And seriously, don't try that at home!)

Think of all you can do in 22 minutes! That's about as long as your favorite DisneyXD TV show. And this guy *held his breath* that long!

But here's the thing, do you think that Stig could hold his breath for 22 minutes the first time he tried?

Doubtful.

Most likely he had to work at it a little at a time. He had to take the time to figure out how to grow his lung capacity. He had to keep at it, even when it got hard, even when he wanted to give up. He knew that working at it would lead to impressive results. And all his work paid off when he set the world record.

There will be times when you want to give up. Standing up for what's right will get hard, but there's a great verse that reminds us it's worth it to keep doing good.

GRAB A BIBLE OR YOUR BIBLE APP AND CHECK OUT GALATIANS 6:9.

"Let us not become tired of doing good. At the right time we will gather a crop if we don't give up."

You may or may not live on a farm, but I bet you can understand what it means to gather a crop. A farmer plants seeds in the spring, takes the time to water the seeds and pull the weeds all summer long until finally in the fall he can go out and gather the crops—the good stuff. It's a long process, but totally worth it when he has baskets and buckets and bushels of delicious food.

The same is true for doing what's right. Even when it gets tough, keep at it. And one day, if you don't give up, you will gather the crops—except instead of big yellow ears of corn and heavy, juicy watermelon, your crops will be things like a really great group of friends you can trust, the respect of others around you, a super-close relationship with God and confidence in yourself.

Just keep at it and practice **standing up**. Soon, showing conviction will be a habit like brushing your teeth, putting your dirty clothes in the hamper or holding your breath under water.

22 minutes! Wow!

DAY 4
1 CORINTHIANS 15:58

You're going to need a friend for this one—or a parent or sibling. Someone you don't mind pushing around a bit. Okay, okay, not that kind of pushing around! It's a harmless game. Here's how it works:

1. Stand facing each other—far enough apart to touch hands with your arms outstretched in front of you.

2. Stand with your feet shoulder-width apart

3. The objective is to knock your opponent off their balance by hitting each other's hands.

4. Stand strong and don't move when your hands hit.

5. First person to take a step to catch their balance is out.

6. Play best of five or as long as you feel like playing!

How did you do? Did you stand strong even when you were getting pushed around?

Not too easy, was it?

Back when people first started following Jesus, there were groups of people who really didn't like it. Religious leaders and government officials were scared that this new "Jesus Movement" was going to take over and leave them with no job or authority. So they tried to stop people from following Jesus. The religious leaders and government officials would hurt those who followed Jesus and try to get them to turn against their faith in Jesus.

So Paul wrote the new Christians a letter to encourage them to keep standing up for their faith.

Check out what he wrote in **1 Corinthians 15:58:**

> *"My dear brothers and sisters, remain strong in the faith. Don't let anything move you. Always give yourselves completely to the work of the Lord. Because you belong to the Lord, you know that your work is not worthless."*

"Don't let anything move you."

That's a pretty big statement, huh? It's hard enough not to move when someone is pushing against you in a game. But what about when you know the right thing to do and someone tries to get you do something different—something that's not right? Do you move away from what you know is right? Or do you stand strong?

> **You know you shouldn't cheat, but someone is asking to copy your answers.**

> **You know your mom doesn't want you to play that video game, but you're at a friend's house, and she might never find out.**

You know that your brother doesn't like you to play with his LEGOs, but he's not home and his bedroom door is open.

Are you going to move?

Every day there are moments when we have to choose if we're going to stand strong or move easily. Sometimes it feels like the easiest choice is to give in and just do what you know is wrong. But in the long run, it's always better to stand firm.

GRAB A SHEET OF PAPER OR AN INDEX CARD. DECORATE IT WITH THESE WORDS:

I WON'T LET ANYTHING MOVE ME.
—1 CORINTHIANS 15:58.

PLACE THIS SOMEWHERE IN YOUR ROOM WHERE IT WILL REMIND YOU TO STAND FOR WHAT'S RIGHT EVEN WHEN YOU DON'T FEEL LIKE STANDING ANYMORE.

Keep standing up! It's worth it!

DAY 5
MARK 1:35 AND LUKE 5:16

You're snug in your bed, cozy and comfortable, maybe even dreaming of riding the roller coasters at Disney World . . . and then it happens.

BEEP BEEP BEEP BEEP BEEP

The alarm.

It jolts you out of bed. You look around and realize that it's still dark outside. But it doesn't matter, you have to get out of bed and get ready for your day.

Let's face it. Having to wake up before the sun is the worst.

Did you know that Jesus used to wake up early, too?

TAKE A QUICK LOOK AT MARK 1:35.

Okay. So why did Jesus wake up early?

And Jesus didn't just do this once.

IF YOU FLIP OVER TO LUKE 5:16, YOU WILL SEE THAT JESUS OFTEN WENT OFF BY HIMSELF TO PRAY.

Jesus was a busy Guy. He had 12 disciples who He cared about and taught all sorts of things. He had crowds of people who wanted His attention. He healed people. He told parables. He taught truths about God's Kingdom.

But even though He was busy, Jesus took time to pray. He knew that He needed to talk to His Father before He headed out to help the crowds of people.

Now, we're all called to be as much like Jesus as possible. Maybe we can't walk on water or enter rooms even when the door is locked. But this one thing—making time to pray—is an easy step towards being like Jesus.

When you pray, you get to talk to God about what's going in your life. You can tell God how you feel. You can talk with Him about what's bothering you. You can even gush about the great things in your life and tell Him what you're thankful for. When you pray, you start to realize that standing up for what's right isn't about making yourself look good; it's about making God look good. Through prayer, God can help you see ways you can **stand up** in your own life.

YOU'RE ALMOST FINISHED WITH THIS BOOK. YOU ONLY HAVE ONE WEEK LEFT. SO GRAB A PEN, PENCIL OR MARKER AND PLAN OUT WHEN YOU'RE GOING TO MAKE TIME TO TALK TO GOD AND READ THE BIBLE OVER THE NEXT WEEK. AND IF YOU WANT TO TAKE THIS HABIT INTO THE COMING WEEKS AND MONTHS, GO AHEAD AND PLAN IT!

Remember, make time to pray before you **stand up**.

	8 AM	9 AM	10 AM	11 AM	NOON	1 PM	2 PM	3 PM	4 PM	5 PM	6 PM	7 PM	8 PM
SUNDAY													
MONDAY													
TUESDAY													
WEDNESDAY													
THURSDAY													
FRIDAY													
SATURDAY													

WEEKEND SEVEN

Did you know that it takes three weeks to make a habit stick? So how can you get in the habit of standing for what's right when there aren't always opportunities every single day to stand up to a bully or choose not to say bad things about someone? It's simple. Make an opportunity to stand up for what's right every day! Truth is, there are hundreds of ways to do the right thing. You just have to get a little creative . . .

It has been one of those mornings. Your alarm didn't go off so you didn't have time to shower. After throwing on the jeans you forgot to wash yesterday and the only shirt left in your drawer (that cheesy one that's about half a size too small), you get downstairs to see you're out of your favorite cereal. With no breakfast and just a couple extra minutes to get to school, you convince your mom to go through the Starbucks drive-thru on the way to school. **You have a few dollars left over from last week's allowance and could use a little pick-me-up.**

You order your usual and when your mom rolls down the window to hand the barista your crumpled dollars, the barista cheerfully calls from the drive-thru window, "The car in front of you paid for your breakfast this morning!"

All of a sudden, your day went from horrible, awful, no good, very bad to terrific, amazing, all good, fantastic!

• •

It's Christmas time again. Most kids look forward to this time of year but you dread it. The last three years have been one big letdown after another. Your dad got fired from his job. Your mom had to drop out of school and start working two jobs. You have to stay in an after school program you hate. **And you know there's no point in asking for presents this Christmas because your mom and dad can barely afford to buy you shoes that fit.**

You do your best to keep a smile on your face so your parents don't know how bummed you are that you're going to be the only kid in your class with nothing to show off when school starts back in January. But the truth is, you would give anything for a video game system like the ones your classmates talk about constantly.

You go to bed Christmas Eve like it's any other night. Maybe you will wake up to a small bag of candy or some new socks. But you don't get your hopes up. **When you get up the next morning, you have to do a double take to believe your eyes.** A large pile of wrapped presents sits under your tree! You run to the pile and sift through tags with your sisters' names and the names of your mom and dad. Finally, a present with your name on it—and it's *heavy*!

You rip the paper from the box and there it is . . . a brand new PlayStation.

• •

Back in August you were *thrilled* to get your very first job at the soft pretzel stand in the mall. Extra cash that's all your own? Yes, please!

But now it's Christmas Eve and you're at the last place anyone in the world wants to be—behind the counter of a soft pretzel stand at the mall. Just last month, you had to leave Thanksgiving dinner early to get to work and face the madness of Black Friday **(which for some reason started on Thursday)**. And when you walked through the door close to midnight, exhausted and beaten down by all the hyped-up holiday shoppers, no one had even saved you a slice of pie.

Now, here you are again, missing your family's Christmas Eve traditions as frantic husbands zigzag from toy store to jewelry store trying to check off their last minute shopping list. Of course no one has time for a real meal in the food court so they all want to grab a quick . . . you guessed it . . . soft pretzel. And so all afternoon and evening you've been serving frazzled customers who scream at you for selling the last cinnamon pretzel to the lady before them or toss change in your face before dashing to the next store or spill sticky soda down your apron because they can't hold the cup and all their bags at once.

You think life couldn't get much worse when one kid comes up, orders politely, looks you in the eye and genuinely says, **"Hey, thanks so much for working on such a crazy day. This pretzel is my favorite part about coming to the mall,"** and then slips a crisp $5 bill into your tip jar.

● ●

Believe it or not, all these things actually happened! Maybe the details were a little different but the acts of kindness, generosity and gratitude were all the same.

In 2011, Courtney DeFeo wrote a blog that started an entire movement. That movement is called **Light 'em Up** and every year, Courtney posts *hundreds* of ideas of ways to stand up and make someone feel really special. One year, a mom paid for the Starbucks order of the car behind her and it continued for *twenty cars*! Another time, a family went to Kmart and had a blast shopping for Christmas gifts for an entire family who wouldn't have presents otherwise. And one girl went around thanking exhausted mall employees a few days before Christmas.

Standing up means knowing and *doing* what God says is right. God says to be kind and generous to others. So what better way to stand up than to commit to doing one small act of kindness that just might make someone else's day?

GET IN THE HABIT OF
STANDING FOR WHAT'S RIGHT.

PETER AND JOHN BEFORE THE SANHEDRIN
ACTS 3:1-9 AND ACTS 4:1-21

For Peter and John, it must have felt like mere moments since Jesus was walking the earth with them. Their minds were surely still spinning with the events of the crucifixion, the resurrection and then Jesus ascending into heaven. He had *died* right in front of their eyes. And then three days later, there He had been, *living again*, right in front of their eyes. And finally, He floated up into the clouds *right before their eyes*!

Undoubtedly, they missed their Friend, but when Jesus rose up to heaven, He hadn't actually left them. A few days later, He sent His Spirit to them. That may sound creepy to you, but Jesus' Spirit wasn't like a scary ghost haunting His friends wherever they went. It was the Holy Spirit living inside of them. Since He was now so close to them, He could communicate His beliefs and desires and thoughts directly to their hearts and minds. **They could always talk to Him, even when they didn't speak out loud. Because He was now always closer to them than He had ever been.**

So one day while on their way to the Temple, Peter and John saw a man begging at the temple gates. The man hadn't been able to walk a single step since he was born more than 40 years before.

"Please, can you spare a few coins?" the man pleaded. "I just need some food . . ."

"I don't have any silver or gold," Peter replied. *"But I'll give you what I do have. In the name of Jesus Christ of Nazareth, get up and walk."*

Peter may not have had this response a few weeks or months earlier, but with the Holy Spirit living inside of him, he knew it was the right thing to do. He was able to respond the way Jesus Himself would have responded.

The crippled man was dubious. "What, are you crazy?" the man asked rhetorically. **But Peter reached out and took the man's hand, who was so surprised he allowed Peter to help him up.** Incredibly, the man's feet and ankles strengthened. His legs supported him! The man's jaw dropped in amazement. "Whoa . . . wow . . . this is amazing!"

The man took his first tentative steps and then walked with increasing confidence right into the Temple courtyards with Peter and John. He began to jump and shout, praising God all the way.

Everyone heard the commotion. People came running to see, and Peter and John were overjoyed by this opportunity to tell all these people about Jesus.

"*Fellow Israelites,*" Peter called out, "*why does this surprise you? Why do you stare at us? It's not as if we've made this man walk by our own power or godliness. The God of our fathers, Abraham, Isaac and Jacob, has done this. God has brought glory to Jesus, who serves him.*"

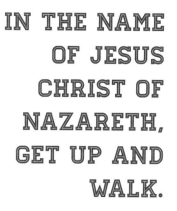

IN THE NAME OF JESUS CHRIST OF NAZARETH, GET UP AND WALK.

The priests and captain of the Temple guard heard the hubbub and marched in to discover what was going on. **They found hundreds of people listening to every word Peter and the rest of the apostles spoke as they explained that Jesus rose from the dead—and that anyone who believes in Him can be resurrected too, and live with God in heaven forever.**

"Because Jesus rose from the dead, that means we can be raised from the dead!" the people were saying.

The priests paled. They didn't agree with this new teaching. And they didn't like that so many people now believed and accepted it. **In their opinion, the situation was quickly becoming dangerous.** "Preposterous!" one of them muttered. "Arrest these men at once and throw them in prison," another commanded the guards. "We'll deal with them in the morning."

The guards quickly surrounded Peter and John. "We've done nothing wrong!" Peter protested.

"We're only speaking as God leads us," John added.

"Yeah, well you can speak to yourself all you want," the guard taunted them. "*In jail.*"

WE'VE DONE NOTHING WRONG!

But even though the religious leaders had silenced Peter and John for a few hours, **they couldn't stop God's good news of salvation from spreading.** Many who had heard the message believed in Jesus. Now, just a short time after Jesus had ascended into heaven, more than 5,000 people were following Him.

Later that night, John shivered in their damp cell behind bars. "Peter, what will they do to us?"

"Does it even matter?" Peter wondered. "John, you saw what happened out there today. Jesus' power can do anything!"

The next morning, Peter and John were hauled out of their cells. "Rise and shine!" the guard commanded. "You want raisins in your gruel?"

"Where are you taking us?" Peter asked.

The guard smirked. "Oh, just a little jaunt . . . *to see the high priest!*"

Peter and John were marched to the Sanhedrin to stand before an imposing group of religious leaders—including the high priest, Annas, along with Caiaphas and other members of the high priest's family.

The man who had been unable to walk stood nearby. He gave them a thumbs up.

"How's it going?" John whispered as they passed.

"I won a dance-off last night!" the man exclaimed, grinning.

Annas narrowed his eyes and tapped his fingertips together. He turned an accusing gaze on Peter and John. **"By what power did you do this?"** Annas demanded, speaking for the religious leaders. **"And through whose name?"**

Peter took a deep breath. He could sense God's Spirit in him, ready to speak through him. "*Rulers and elders of the people!*" he called out. "*Are you asking us to explain our actions today? Do you want to know why we were kind to a man who couldn't walk? Are you asking how he was healed?*"

The religious leaders exchanged annoyed glances. They were supposed to be asking the questions. Not Peter!

"*Then listen to this, you and all of the people of Israel!*" Peter continued. "*You nailed Jesus Christ of Nazareth to the cross. But God raised him from the dead.* **It is through Jesus' name that this man stands healed in front of you.**"

The man who had been unable to walk couldn't resist doing a dance. "Stands?" he laughed. "More than that, man. Walks. Jumps. Hops, leaps, dances!"

Peter kept right on going. "*Scripture says that Jesus is 'the stone you builders did not accept. But it has become the most important stone of all.' You can't be saved by believing in anyone else.*"

Annas was mad enough to start hopping himself. He leaned over

and whispered. "They don't have any education. How in the blazes do they know these things?"

"Sounds like they really *have* been with Jesus," Caiaphas pointed out.

"Not helping!" Annas growled. Then he took a deep breath and raised his voice to the crowd. "You—Peter, John, and, um . . . Dancing Dude. Leave us. We'll call you back when we're ready."

As soon as Peter and John left, the religious leaders began to argue.

"We have to shut them up!" Annas declared.

"But everyone saw that man get up and walk," Caiaphas pointed out. "We can't say it didn't happen."

"More than 40 years old and never walked a step in his life!" a leader with a beaky nose exclaimed.

Annas glared at him. "Not helping."

Caiaphas crossed his arms. "You're in charge. Just tell them to stop."

"Did you see the dance moves that guy had?" the beaky-nosed leader inquired, toes tapping. "Think he could teach me?"

"*Not helping!*" Annas thundered, and then controlled his voice once more. **"We have to warn these men. They must never speak to anyone in Jesus' name again."**

The leaders called Peter and John back into the room. The two men met Annas' eyes squarely without flinching. Annas fidgeted under their direct gaze and finally spoke, almost defiantly. "We've decided," he announced. "You must never speak or teach again in Jesus' name!"

Peter and John stood firm and shook their heads. "*Which is right from God's point of view?*" Peter questioned. "*Should we listen to you? Or should we listen to God?*"

"*There's nothing else we can do,*" John added. **"*We have to speak about the things we've seen and heard.*"** He gestured to the window. They could see the man who had been unable to walk, now doing a little jig for the crowd.

SHOULD WE LISTEN TO YOU? OR SHOULD WE LISTEN TO GOD?

Annas groaned and shut his eyes. It seemed there was nothing he could do to stop these men from telling everyone about Jesus. He fixed them with one last glare. "Just. Don't. Do it!" he hissed through clenched teeth.

Unable to decide how to punish Peter and John, the religious leaders let them go. As Peter and John left the Sanhedrin, their dancing friend gave them a high five. "Praise Jesus, man!"

"Praise Jesus!" they replied.

Peter and John didn't stay silent as Annas had told them to do. In fact, they continued to share about Jesus with everyone they met, fueled by the amazing truth that Jesus is alive.

DAY 1
ACTS 4:1-21

The Bible is full of stories that will **blow your mind**. You think zombie movies and exorcisms are a new thing? Oh no, people rose from the dead in the Bible. Demons were cast out of people in the Bible. You think these reality shows where people have to eat bugs and walk across ropes courses are intense? What about surviving on locusts in the desert? What about fighting off a pack of hungry lions with your bare hands? What about going up against a WWE-type giant with a sling shot? It's all in the Bible. (You should read it sometime.)

But one of the hundreds of mind-blowing stories comes from the book of Acts. And it tells us about the time Jesus' friends, Peter and John, met a guy who had never been able to walk. Peter told him to get up and start walking . . . and the man did! That's right, Jesus wasn't the only person in the Bible to heal others. Peter did it too, with the help of the Holy Spirit.

What?! Now, *that* had to be incredible to see.

But apparently everyone wasn't so thrilled to see this miracle in Jesus' name. In fact, the religious leaders were pretty angry that Peter and John kept going on and on about Jesus. The religious leaders didn't believe Jesus is alive and still working. So they threw Peter and John in jail and threatened to have them killed if they *didn't stop talking about Jesus*!

But Peter and John were just getting started.

TAKE A LOOK AT WHAT THEY SAID IN ACTS 4:18-20!

They showed conviction and said that no matter what, they would always talk about Jesus!

Whoa now! Peter and John didn't care that they could be *killed*. They just shrugged and basically said, "Do what you want. We won't keep our mouths shut."

Do you think they could have stood so strong if they didn't know Jesus was alive?

No. Way.

That's what's so amazing. Jesus dying and God raising Him back to life isn't just a nice story.

It's true. It's fact. It really, actually happened.

GRAB YOUR BIBLE AND CHECK OUT THESE VERSES WRITTEN BY PEOPLE WHO ACTUALLY SAW JESUS ALIVE OR KNEW PEOPLE FIRST HAND WHO HAD SEEN HIM ALIVE AFTER BEING CRUCIFIED AND BURIED.

LUKE 24:6
ACTS 4:33
1 CORINTHIANS 15:3-4
1 PETER 1:3

Jesus is alive. For real. That means everything He said is true, and that He is more powerful than any difficulty you will ever face. It means that **you can stand for what's right . . . because Jesus is alive!**

DAY 2
2 THESSALONIANS 2:13-17

Have you ever tried to run on the beach when the sand is really loose and dry? **CLOSE YOUR EYES AND PICTURE WHAT IT'S LIKE OR WHAT YOU THINK IT MIGHT BE LIKE.**

Okay, you can open them again. (Wait. I guess if you are reading this you already have . . .)

Anyway, it's really tough to get anywhere, isn't it? Your feet sink in and slide around. You can't get any traction, so you end up working extra hard just to keep your balance. You don't have solid ground to stand on.

Sometimes it can feel like that in your everyday life, too. A friend sends you a link to a website you know your mom and dad wouldn't want you to visit. But your friend says the video is *super* funny. Suddenly you're sliding around. You know you shouldn't click, but you're just about to do it anyway. **You need something solid to stand on.**

That's when knowing what God says is super important.

PICK UP YOUR BIBLE OR CLICK ON YOUR BIBLE APP AND READ 2 THESSALONIANS 2:13-17.

Check out what sort of foundation God gives us to stand on.

Jesus has done some amazing things for you. He loves you and chose you to be His friend. He's growing you to be holy—more like Him. He has given you comfort and He has given you hope. And take a look at that last verse: He makes you strong in every good thing you do and say!

So next time you face a slippery situation, hold onto these truths. **Remember that you can stand up because of what Jesus did for you.**

In fact, you can decorate these awesome kicks below to remind you that God will help you **stand up** for what's right. What would you like them to look like? What would you want to have written on them?

GO CRAZY AND COLOR 'EM UP!

DAY 3
ACTS 6:8 – 7:60

Is there a book you've read over and over again but it never gets old? Or maybe a movie you could watch every. single. day? Write the title here:

[ ]

One of the best things about re-reading your favorite book or re-watching a movie you love is that you know how it ends. You know what's going to happen to the characters. So you don't panic when they face circumstances that seem impossibly difficult.

Did you know that the same thing is true for *your* story? Yep. It sure is. **If you believe in what Jesus did for you and choose to be His friend, then you do know the end of your story: Everything will be made right, and you'll get to live forever with Jesus!**

A man named Stephen knew this, and it gave him the strength to stand up in a *big* way.

YOU CAN READ STEPHEN'S STORY IN ACTS 6:8–7:60. (IT'S A LITTLE LONG, BUT IT'S WORTH IT IF YOU WANT TO READ THE WHOLE THING!)

Here's the quick version. Stephen was arrested for talking about Jesus. He could have lied his way out, said he didn't really follow Jesus and gone home. But he didn't. He was filled with the Holy Spirit who gave him the courage to start telling God's story—the *whole* story. Stephen connected all the dots that went from the beginning of the Old Testament right to Jesus. The people who arrested him were furious. They ended up putting Stephen to death, all because of his faith in Jesus.

Throughout all of it, Stephen had courage and showed conviction. *Stephen could stand up because he knew God's story*—how God loved His people and had made a way to rescue them. Stephen knew that *even if he died*, God would rescue him. So he was able to stand strong, even when people wanted to kill him.

You probably won't face people who want to throw stones at you but when you know and remember God's story, you'll be able to stand up, because you know how your story ends. You'll know that even if you get teased or miss out on something fun, everything will be made right some day.

Think about the part YOU get to play in God's Big Story. What sort of Super Hero will you be? **GRAB SOME MARKERS OR COLORED PENCILS OR CRAYONS AND DECORATE THE ILLUSTRATION ON THE NEXT PAGE. MAKE YOURSELF INTO A SUPERHERO THAT COULD PLAY A PART IN THE STORY GOD IS TELLING!**

PLAY A
PART IN
GOD'S BIG
STORY!

DAY 4
ROMANS 8:37-39

Did you know that some people would panic just picking up this book? That's because they're afraid of *all* books. Seriously! A fear of books is called "bibliophobia." (If you have bibliophobia, you have no idea how proud you should be for making it this far.)

In fact, people can be afraid of just about anything, from big scary stuff to silly little things. TAKE A LOOK AT THE SUPER-HUGE WORDS FOR DIFFERENT KINDS OF FEARS ON THE LEFT, AND SEE IF YOU CAN MATCH THEM UP WITH WHAT THEY MEAN ON THE RIGHT.

Chronophobia	**fear of technology**
Dromophobia	**fear of darkness**
Ergophobia	**fear of fire**
Heliophobia	**fear of work**
Lygophobia	**fear of animals**
Pyrophobia	**fear of strangers**
Technophobia	**fear of time**
Xenophobia	**fear of crossing streets**
Zoophobia	**fear of the sun**

Crazy what people can be afraid of, isn't it?

Truth is, we're all afraid sometimes—especially when it comes to standing up for what's right. In some situations, it's easy. But other times, standing up can feel just plain scary.

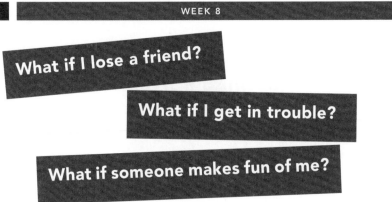

What if I lose a friend?

What if I get in trouble?

What if someone makes fun of me?

Sometimes, these things might actually happen. But there's one thing that will never happen. One thing that will never change. Take a look at the following Bible passages. They're from the book of Romans, chapter eight, verses 37-39.

> *No! In all these things we are more than winners! We owe it all to Christ, who has loved us. I am absolutely sure that not even death or life can separate us from God's love. Not even angels or demons, the present or the future, or any powers can separate us. Not even the highest places or the lowest, or anything else in all creation can separate us. Nothing at all can ever separate us from God's love. That's because of what Christ Jesus our Lord has done.*

Bottom line is this: **no matter what happens, God will still love you.** If you believe in what Jesus did for you, you will still live with Him forever. There is no person and no thing on this earth that can ever change that. So you know that **you can stand up because God's got your back**.

Just remember that next time you're tempted toward bufonophobia—fear of toads!

chronophobia – time; dromophobia – crossing streets; ergophobia – work; heliophobia - the sun; lygophobia – darkness; pyrophobia; fire; technophobia – technology; xenophobia – strangers; zoophobia – animals]

DAY 5
JOHN 16:33

Ever had a morning when you woke up with a knot in your stomach . . . and just getting out of bed and walking out of your front door seemed like the hardest thing in the world?

Maybe there's a kid on your soccer team who always makes fun of you.

Or maybe a boy in your class has been bugging you to let him copy your homework.

Maybe you're even dreading going to a friend's sleepover because she always says mean things about everyone else.

Whatever the situation, it may feel like it's up to you to fix it. Like you've got to grit your teeth and just get through it. And you're not sure you've got what it takes to stand strong.

But here's the thing: you're not in this alone. Someone has already faced the tough stuff for you! Take a look at what Jesus says in John 16:33:

> *"I have told you these things, so that you can have peace because of me. In this world you will have trouble. But be encouraged! I have won the battle over the world."*

Jesus has just finished telling His friends how much God loves them and how He will help them any time they ask. His friends can have peace and confidence because Jesus is about to stand up to the most difficult thing in the world—death!—and beat it.

Jesus is bigger and stronger than anything you're going to face when you walk out of your front door—whether it's a bully on your sports team or friends who want you to make fun of someone else. Jesus has overcome every trouble in this world, and He will help you do the same when you ask.

It's easy to know that . . . and just as easy to forget!

So today, make yourself a cool reminder that **you can stand up, because Jesus already has**.

FIND A NOTECARD AND YOUR FAVORITE ART SUPPLIES, WHETHER IT'S MARKERS OR PAINT AND GLITTER. NOW WRITE OUT JOHN 16:33, DECORATE THE CARD IN A SUPER BRIGHT, EYE-CATCHING WAY, AND TAPE IT TO THE WALL OR DOOR FRAME WHERE YOU'LL SEE IT EVERY TIME YOU LEAVE THE HOUSE.

WEEKEND EIGHT

Knowing that Jesus died and then came back to life gives us the courage to stand for what's right. The fact that Jesus is alive means He really is the Son of God, He really did die for our sins and He really did make it possible for us to all be with Him in heaven one day! And that kind of awesome news is too cool to not share.

Elisabeth and Jim Elliott devoted their lives to sharing the good news that Jesus paid the price for our sins so we can live with God forever. They moved to Ecuador as missionaries to share God's love with the Quichua Indians, when Jim was killed by some of the members of a neighboring tribe. While most people would return home and never go back, Elisabeth forgave the tribe members who killed her husband. She spent two years sharing God's love with the Aucas people, many of whom came to trust in Christ.

www.lonelyplanet.com/ecuador/quito/images

Jim Elliot grew up in Portland, Oregon. His parents had firm Christian beliefs and Jim attended church throughout his childhood. In school, Jim was known as a talented speaker and one time even used his knowledge of Scripture to explain his reasoning for not attending a party he knew he shouldn't go to. **(Talk about using God's Word to stand up for what's right!)**

While in college at Wheaton, Jim met Elisabeth Howard. They were instantly attracted to one another. They held the same beliefs and had the same passion for sharing the incredible news of Jesus. They were still very young and had a lot of important things going for them in life so they didn't pursue a relationship right away.

But when Jim packed up and moved to Ecuador to be a missionary, he and Elisabeth couldn't stand to be apart. When they were 26 years old, they got married in the city of Quito, Ecuador. Jim had been working with a group of Quichua Indians in Ecuador and soon heard of an even more savage people group called the Huaorani. **Jim wanted everyone to know God's love and follow the teachings of Jesus so he and a few of the other missionaries began making contact with the Huaorani people.**

They started by flying over their village in a plane. They spoke to them with a loudspeaker and dropped gifts down in a basket. Soon, Jim helped to build a base close to the Huaorani people and even had friendly encounters with them. Jim and the other missionaries were encouraged by this and believed they were getting through to the group of savages. However, ten Huaorani warriors soon came and killed Jim and four of his missionary companions.

Elisabeth Elliot was left a widow, raising their infant daughter in Ecuador. **Elisabeth could have given up and returned home to New England but she didn't. Elisabeth stayed in Ecuador and continued to stand up and spread the good news of God's love.** Even though they had killed her husband and left her only daughter without a father, Elisabeth hadn't given up on the Huaorani people.

Elisabeth dedicated her time to learning the language and culture of the Huaorani people and two years after they murdered her husband, Elisabeth and her three-year-old daughter went to live with the savages. The Huaorani people gave Elisabeth a tribal name meaning "woodpecker." Because of Elisabeth's relentless conviction and great act of forgiveness, the Huaorani people allowed her to share with them about Jesus. Many members of the tribe were converted to Christianity and the murder rate among the Huaorani people dropped by 90%!

Because of Elisabeth's conviction to stand up and spread God's message of love to even the darkest places in the world, an entire people group came to know the story of Jesus.

WE CAN STAND FOR WHAT'S RIGHT BECAUSE JESUS IS ALIVE.